Dignity at Work

Bullying in the workplace is now a recognised problem, and a cause for major concern. Victims stand to lose their self-esteem, their health and even their careers. Organisations that do not endeavour to put an end to this behaviour lose productivity, profits and their good reputations.

Dignity at Work is derived from the author's many years of experience working with organisations of all sizes and at all levels. This book outlines practical guidelines essential to organisations that want to combat bullying in the workplace, and psychologists and professional counsellors working with those organisations. It provides:

- The tools to identify bullying behaviour
- Expertise to create new policies and integrate them into corporate culture
- Confidence to know when and how to intervene practically and therapeutically
- The skills required to know when to seek external help from professional counsellors
- Psychologists and counsellors with advice on how to transfer their skills to organisations as independent contractors

Bullying will no longer be tolerated, and organisations must create environments that do not support mistreatment. This book provides managers, human resource staff and professional counsellors with the skills required to be able to recognise when a problem exists, and deal with it effectively.

Pauline Rennie Peyton is an integrative psychotherapist and a chartered psychologist. Since presenting her first paper on 'Bullying at Work' in 1995, she has built a reputation as a pre-eminent expert in this field. As a consultant to organisations large and small, she assists in policy writing and implementation, training, investigating, mediating and counselling the victims and perpetrators of bullying. Her website is www.renniepeyton.com

Dignity at Work

Eliminate Bullying and Create a Positive Working Environment

Pauline Rennie Peyton

Routledge
Taylor & Francis Group

LONDON AND NEW YORK

First published 2003 by Brunner-Routledge
27 Church Road, Hove, East Sussex, BN3 2FA

Simultaneously published in the USA and Canada
by Brunner-Routledge
29 West 35th Street, New York, NY 10001

Reprinted 2005 by Routledge
27 Church Road, Hove, East Sussex, BN3 2FA
270 Madison Avenue, New York, NY 10016

Routledge is an imprint of the Taylor & Francis Group

Copyright © 2003 Pauline Rennie Peyton

Typeset in Times by Mayhew Typesetting, Rhayader, Powys
Printed and bound in Great Britain by TJ International, Padstow, Cornwall
Paperback cover design by Lisa Dynan

This publication has been produced with paper manufactured to strict
environmental standards and with pulp derived from sustainable forests.

British Library Cataloguing in Publication Data
A catalogue record for this book is available from the British Library

Library of Congress Cataloging-in-Publication Data
Rennie Peyton, Pauline, 1952–
    Dignity at work : eliminate bullying and create a positive working
environment / Pauline Rennie Peyton.– 1st ed.
        p. cm.
Includes bibliographical references and index.
    ISBN 1-58391-237-1 (hbk) – ISBN 1-58391-238-X (pbk.)
1. Bullying. 2. Bullying in the workplace. I. Title.

    BF637.B85R46 2003
    658.3'82–dc21

                                                2003011070

ISBN 1-58391-237-1 (hbk)
ISBN 1-58391-238-X (pbk)

Contents

About the author

Pauline Rennie Peyton is an integrative psychotherapist and a chartered psychologist with many years of experience working in organisations and specialising in the field of human relationships. This includes harassment and bullying.

She gave her first conference paper on 'Bullying at Work' in 1995 and since then has accumulated a vast wealth of experience in the field. As a psychologist-consultant, she advises on policy writing and delivers training programmes to organisational personnel who want to know not only how to prevent but also deal with these unacceptable behaviours when they arise. She also trains harassment investigators, carries out investigations and works both with the bullied and those accused of bullying. Using creative team-building techniques she helps organisations to heal after distressing and disruptive events have taken place. She trained in mediation in 1998. Since that time she has worked as a mediator in organisations with both pairs and groups.

Pauline Rennie Peyton has a busy clinical practice working as a counselling psychologist both privately and for major employee assistance programme (EAP) providers. In both capacities, as a trained mediator, she also resolves disputes and issues that arise between two or more people. Because of her substantial experience in working with trauma, the EAP component of her work has included critical-incident debriefing and post-traumatic stress counselling in the aftermath of catastrophes such as the Paddington rail crash and 11 September.

She considers that trauma from bullying at work is no less debilitating for some people than being involved in the major traumatic events that are given more press coverage and understood to be traumatic by the world at large.

Preface
Who this book is for

This manual is written for anyone who has responsibility for others in the workplace. Its chief aim is to provide practical and useful solutions not only to managers and Human Resources professionals working within organisations, but also to counsellors and psychotherapists who are transferring their experience and skills from the outside to corporate settings and situations.

In particular, the manual offers frameworks for policies – and procedures for putting those policies into practice. It also reveals the ways to break down the psychological barriers that prevent highly competent professionals working more efficiently in organisations.

For counsellors and psychologists who are trying to expand their work-base into organisations, the material in the following chapters provides both the practical and theoretical means of enabling health professionals and organisational personnel to work side by side with a common goal of improving the workplace.

With the above in mind, the manual has been divided into two sections: Part 1 contains information for Human Resources personnel, managers, smaller employers and anyone who must deal with bullying at work; Part 2 is specifically for counsellors, psychologists or psychotherapists who, as outside experts, are importing their specialist skills into the organisation.

Many multinationals and other large organisations already have well-formulated policies in place. This manual may therefore be invaluable to those enterprises that employ fewer people (less than 50) who up until now have never thought these policies might be relevant to them. Of course, they are neither exempt from the law nor impervious to the dangers of an environment in which bullying is unchecked.

Acknowledgements

Thank you to all those people who have let me into their lives to share their pain and suffering through bullying at work.

Many, many thanks to my supporters and supervisors, Professors Michael Carroll and Diana Shmukler.

Thank you to Ian Stewart for teaching me to think and use transactional analysis (TA) as a tool for my work. Thank you to my friends Sue Culley and Leslie Holland, who have taught me so much about this field. My deep appreciation as well to others also involved in this work who have generously encouraged me, given me material and shared the fruit of their own labours. Thank you, Chris Ball, Hilary Tivey, Charlotte Raynor, Hedwig Petri, Tim Field and Helge Hoel – to name a few.

To Tony, thank you for being one of the people who showed me that bullying is unacceptable, destructive and a waste of some of our best talents. I'm happy that you have proved to us all that there is life after being so badly treated.

My love and appreciation to my number-one fan and precious husband Charlie.

Thank you to my friends whose encouragement makes everything possible.

And, to Lainey, to Gill and to Anthony, without whose never-ending patience this project would not have been completed, thank you, thank you, thank you.

Part 1

A handbook for Human Resources personnel, managers and corporate executives

Chapter 1

Why is bullying an important issue?

Behaviours that were still tolerated right up until the last decade of the last century are not necessarily acceptable now. Yet, in the face of change, even obvious and welcome change, for most of us the feeling is one of trepidation.

Coming to terms with my own resistance to change has given me some understanding of how the same phenomenon operates within organisations and the people inside them.

The prospect of change is no less difficult for companies than it is for individuals. Indeed, sometimes it is even harder. In spite of that, it is now time to stop paying lip service to the notion of dignity at work and start taking it seriously. The myriad reasons will be explained in the following chapters; suffice it to say for now that the general population is becoming increasingly aware of bullying in the workplace (as more cases are litigated in the courts and exposed in the national press). Together with this awareness also comes the understanding of just how dangerous and unacceptable this behaviour is. And yet, for all this exposure and the ongoing research, there is still not enough information 'out there' primarily because people are not recognising bullying behaviour when they see it and are not acknowledging its inappropriateness in today's business world. Most of us working in the field agree that we do not know the extent to which people are suffering at other people's hands.

Since Andrea Adams published her book *Bullying at Work* in 1992, research has been undertaken in this country and abroad, TV documentaries have been made, books written, and legal action against employers won. Yet, in spite of the greater awareness, bullying and harassment continue in the workplace, largely unabated.

Speaking at a conference sponsored by the British Trade Union MSF, Adams (1994a) said:

> Isn't it amazing the Employment Secretary has stated that the Government deplores workplace bullying, that it wishes to see employers adopt the most modern management practices, and would always encourage employers to treat their employees with the consideration they are due. If this were truly the case, how does one explain the apparent failure of so many organisations to protect their people from one of the most stressful, destructive, humiliating and financially undermining forces at large in the British workplace?

Sadly, she could give the same speech nine years on, since little has changed.

Cherie Booth QC, wife of the current British Prime Minister, speaking at a conference organised by ChildLine – the telephone help-line and charity – stated 'Bullying doesn't stop at the school gates, it goes on after school and it goes on into University. It goes on into work and it even goes on into the family. It is a real issue at the heart of our culture.'

As a society we are becoming more and more 'me-centred' and it is therefore not surprising that people treat each other with less and less respect. This is evident wherever we look: at the supermarket, the cinema, the bus stop or on the television!

We see children abuse each other on their way to and from school; we watch them push their way in front of the elderly waiting to get onto buses. We read of teachers being bullied and physically attacked by pupils and their parents. We hear of parents bullying their children and even of children bullying their parents.

Much of my work consists of short-term employee assistance programme counselling, in which I deal with diverse issues both personal and work-based. In the course of these assignments I have become increasingly aware of the effects of bullying and harassment both in the workplace and in people's private lives.

The prime element that seems to be missing in these interpersonal relationships is *respect*. Therefore, at its most basic, what I am advocating is that the key to improved relationships is respect. In this book, however, I am concentrating solely on workplace relationships.

It is sad when people do not expect to be treated with respect either because of an inherited belief system or by being worn down by a particular organisational culture. For example, I think of the woman who said, 'I'm only the typist', or the man who shrugged, 'I am only the odd-job man'. The truth is that both these people were successful and did their jobs professionally and with good grace. But unfortunately too few people respect their own – and others' – positive qualities but measure success only in terms of status, pay cheque and the car they drive.

Tim Field's helpline – The National Workplace Bullying Advice Line – had 5,156 enquiries and 4,598 cases of bullying during the period January 1996 to May 2001. This is just one agency. It is also important to remember that these statistics represent just the reported cases – most people, if they talk about it at all, tell only their families and friends. Usually they tell no one; they just leave their jobs. Clearly, the effects of workplace bullying are felt not only by the employee but by the employer as well.

In fact, the Health and Safety Executive claims that bullying is responsible for 30–50 per cent of all stress-related illness in the workplace, resulting in poor morale and productivity and higher staff turnover. The cost to employers is 80 million working days and up to £2 billion in lost revenue every year.

This book is not only about making people aware of the dark or shadowy side of organisational life, it also aims to guide people into doing something about it. Previously it may have been only in large corporations that the way in which people are treated – and the need to take action on bullying – was recognised. However, this is no longer the case and all employers of people have to be aware of their duty of care towards every one of their employees.

Many readers will be familiar with the following rationale: 'We don't worry about policies here. We are too small and, besides, I have run this show for 20 years and nothing like this has ever happened before.' Needless to say, this comment was made by the managing director of a small company whose idea of management was encapsulated in another of his favourite sayings, 'If you don't like it, you know where the door is.'

Fortunately for people who are vulnerable, this attitude is no longer sustainable, as we have seen reflected over the last few years in successful litigation. For example, Oberhardt (1998) reports a case in which a woman sued the owners of a newspaper at which she had worked. She claimed to have suffered a psychiatric breakdown as a direct result of the abuse from her manager who had berated her with foul language, boasted of his ability to reduce women to tears and made false allegations against her. The judge found that the manager exceeded the parameters of his authority and agreed that the woman suffered a serious permanent psychiatric injury because of her treatment.

Results such as these confirm that unfair treatment of employees is now beginning to be taken more seriously in the mainstream. However, it is also true to say that most cases do not reach the press because companies being sued normally prefer to settle them out of court, thereby avoiding not only the adverse publicity but also the more comprehensive financial and legal consequences of losing the action.

Organisations that do not take the fair treatment of their staff seriously run the risk of having an unmotivated workforce, high levels of absences due to sickness, high rates of staff turnover and the threat of litigation. The ultimate consequence is the damage to their reputations as employers. This, in turn, can make recruitment more difficult and profit margins smaller, especially in areas where populations are less dense and the potential pool from which to attract a workforce is below the national average.

Nevertheless, all organisations need to identify, take responsibility for and resolve conflicts when they first occur. They need to ask questions such as 'How can this situation be resolved swiftly, legally and with the least harm to all concerned?'

Many organisations have slick, empathetic mission statements and well-constructed company policies, which are neither read nor put into practice. Within your own organisation, how many employees know what the company mission statement says? How many believe it?

As an employee assistance professional who has been called in to deal with hundreds of short-term clients, I begin by asking 'What does your company policy say regarding harassment and bullying?' In my experience, the reply I get most often is that they do not even know whether one exists. Indeed, they are often surprised to see, once they get hold of a copy of the policy, that the behaviour they are enduring at the hands of others is not acceptable within their organisation.

When I run workshops or present papers at conferences, I usually ask the delegates to think about a time when they were either the person being bullied or a witness to incidents of bullying.

To the question 'Do you bully people or have you done so in the past?' the surprising response is normally that 99 per cent admit to having been involved in some way.

Human Resources personnel are themselves by no means immune to the attentions of bullies. In a survey carried out by Robinson (1999) in *Personnel Today*, the magazine for Human Resources professionals, more than 70 per cent of the 331 personnel professionals involved in the survey reported having been bullied in their jobs. One third reported that they were currently being bullied and two out of five reported having witnessed a colleague being bullied. These people are at a particular disadvantage since the only person they can turn to is their immediate supervisor – and yet in 64 per cent of cases the bully is their immediate supervisor.

This only reinforces the necessity to have clear, unambiguous policies about workplace bullying and, no less crucially, systems and procedures in place to work alongside them.

Chapter 2

A background to bullying at work

What constitutes harassment and bullying?

The terms 'harassment' and 'bullying', and the differences between them, often confuse people. Although the terms are defined in greater detail in Chapter 3, both bullying and harassment consist of behaviours that are unwelcome, inappropriate, offensive, unreciprocated and irrelevant to work performance. Bullying is a specific form of harassment and is insidious by nature in the sense that it usually develops gradually (sometimes even imperceptibly until the pattern is established), but it has a cumulative, entrapping effect on the victim.

People can be harassed on the grounds of race, ethnic origin, nationality or skin colour, sex, sexual orientation, religious or political convictions, membership of (or non-membership of) trade unions and other apolitical organisations, status within the organisation, physical appearance (including disabilities), status as an ex-offender or as someone suffering (or suspected to be suffering) from HIV/AIDS, education or just for being different. They can even be harassed for their willingness to stand up and challenge harassment.

However, we have reached a stage in organisational development where people have a right to expect to be treated well in their place of work.

In 1995, the TUC passed a motion condemning 'the spread of bullying and hectoring management styles which intimidate, humiliate and dehumanize employees.'

Research on bullying at work

Back in 1956, Seyle stated that stress is 'the body's response to troublesome situations, events or thoughts'. It is hardly surprising, therefore, that being bullied at work has been found to be a major stressor.

Leymann (1990) put the effects of bullying under four main headings:

1 *Social* – social isolation, stigmatising, voluntary unemployment, social maladjustment.
2 *Social/psychological* – loss of coping resources. Petri (1997) calls this effect 'breakdown of the mental nerve system'.
3 *Psychological* – desperation and total helplessness, considerable rage about lack of legal remedies, great anxiety and despair.
4 *Psychosomatic and psychiatric* – depression, hyperactivity, compulsion, suicide and psychosomatic illnesses.

Leymann (1993) carried out his research in Sweden on people seeking treatment for workplace-acquired illnesses of a psychological and psychosomatic nature. Based on over 500 cases in 1990, Leymann describes the medical history of the bullied victim. He found that after several days, symptoms of stress such as disturbed sleep and mild depression were in evidence and observed that over a period of six months this led to post-traumatic stress disorder (PTSD). His clinical evidence shows that after a year the victim is diagnosed with generalised anxiety disorder (GAD) syndrome; after two to four years the condition becomes chronic and has, therefore, developed into a psychiatric illness. Later, Rayner (1997) quoted Leymann's statistics that one in seven adult suicides in Sweden is the result of workplace bullying.

This work was reinforced by Bjorkqvist *et al.* (1994) who used the 'Work Harassment Scale' (WHS) on university employees and found that without exception victims claimed to have experienced feelings of depression, anxiety and aggressiveness as a direct consequence of the treatment to which they had been exposed. In all cases there were reports of insomnia, various nervous symptoms, melancholy, apathy, lack of concentration and sociophobia. Depression, anxiety and aggression scores of harassed employees were roughly one-third higher on the WHS scale than those of their colleagues. The conclusions of the study were that victims of harassment do suffer from PTSD.

Einarssen *et al.* (1994), quoted in Rayner (1997), found correlation between a high occurrence of bullying and 'leadership style' (in Scandinavian literature this refers to a lack of leadership), role conflict and work control. Insufficient work control and high levels of role conflict are seen to act as precursors to bullying. Those who are perceived as being responsible for the respective levels of control and role conflict may, where these levels cause problems, be seen as bullies.

Bullies are generally afraid of not being sufficiently in control and are often described by their teams as 'control freaks'. A bully's understanding of the concept of leadership is frequently distorted, which is why – instead of guiding their teams and fostering cohesiveness – their behaviour is over-controlling. This has psychological and physiological effects on their people.

Von Eckardstein *et al.* (1995) discusses how these detriments to psychological well-being lead to an impaired quality of life and a higher risk of psychosomatic illness. He suggests it has negative effects on an individual's health and lifestyle (e.g., bad diet, addictions such as alcohol, increased conflicts and an increased risk of becoming ill).

Randall (1997) refers to the 'noxious stimuli' received from the bully that result in the persistent re-experiencing of the trauma. His findings are based on in-depth case studies.

Petri's (1996) unpublished research showed similar outcomes. She suggests that the publication of case studies has helped bring the issue of workplace bullying into the open. This has certainly been the material that journalists have been attracted to and reported on in the general press.

In their research, Beasley *et al.* (1997) found a ripple effect from workplace bullying. The victims 'lose interest in their families, be[come] irritable and even aggressive towards those whom they love'.

In line with this view, Petri (1998), in unpublished research, cites a case in which the family's housing was linked to the bullied husband's job. Here, the whole family was not only affected but indeed devastated by the impact of the employer's behaviour.

In Austria and Germany, a number of studies on 'mobbing' – another term for bullying – were undertaken. Zapf *et al.* (1995) in one study, and Niedl (1995) in another, investigated the mental-health effects of mobbing on employees. Both studies used a battery of psychological instruments (including the Leymann Inventory of

Psychological Terrorisation) as well as control groups. The findings of the two separate studies were similar in that they showed significant differences between the mobbing samples and the control groups.

Zapf *et al.* agree that mobbing is an extreme form of work-based social stressor. They report that 54 per cent of cases received medical treatment.

Groeblinghoff and Becker (1996) refer to mobbing as an unethical disorder of communication and an extreme psychosocial stressor, the effects of which frequently cause severe symptoms of combined psychological and physical illness. They concluded that these symptoms impair the victims' vitality, overall potential, creativity and productivity.

The results of their research through case studies were comparable with other researchers' conclusions. They put forward the following list of outcomes: depression, obsession, agitation and blockage, a resigned attitude, moderate cognitive disturbances with automatically recurring thoughts, irritability, inner unrest, insomnia, substance abuse and suicidal tendencies.

In 1998 Cooper *et al.* listed mental symptoms of stress. According to Petri (1998) this list shows remarkable similarities to the symptoms reported by workplace-abuse victims. The relationships at work were then, and are now, of prime importance. What we now call bullying was ten years ago referred to as 'office politics' or 'personality conflicts'. Petri concludes that in ten years the behaviour hasn't changed but has merely been relabelled.

Petri (1998) quotes from a booklet issued by The European Foundation for the Improvement of Living and Working Conditions containing advice on how to recognise stress. 'Most of us experience anxiety, depression, uneasiness, restlessness and fatigue. Stress at work can also make some of us start smoking more or overeating, seeking comfort in alcohol or taking unnecessary risks at work or in traffic. Many of these reactions lead to disease and premature death. Suicide is one of many examples' (Kompier and Levi, 1994).

Cooper (1993) advises organisations to consider what they can provide to combat workplace stress, not what they can do to alleviate it.

People who are stressed may continue to turn up for work and perform poorly. Cox (1993) refers to this as 'presenteeism', which was defined in a Health and Safety Information Bulletin of May 1996 as 'being physically present at work but mentally absent'.

In their 1995 personal injury firm study, Earnshaw and Cooper (1996) found that the majority of workplace stress claims were not due to work overload or long working hours. Instead, they found the most prevalent trigger for stress injury was alleged to be bullying in one shape or another (variously described as persecution/victimisation/bullying/pressure management). The results were:

Trigger	No. of occurrences
Bullying	13
Hours of work	6
Duties/workload	6

The most common injury was a nervous breakdown (17 cases) followed by depression (9 cases).

Consequently, Earnshaw and Cooper reported that up to a third of UK stress-related employment legal cases are primarily as a result of workplace bullying. The then Director-General of the UK Health and Safety Executive, Jenny Bacon, put the cost of stress at work at £4.5 billion (*People Management*, 27 June 1996, p.14).

Rayner (1997) advocates the logic of thinking about bullying in terms of stress, this being compatible with the Cox (1978) transactional stress model, which views stress as an active and dynamic process between a person and his/her environment. In this context stress is seen as the discrepancy between the perceived capability and the perceived demands when approaching a stressful situation. In this way, the bully both undermines a person's perceived capability and increases the demands they perceive being made of them in work situations. February 2000 saw the publication of a survey carried out by the University of Manchester Institute of Science and Technology (UMIST), supported by the TUC and CBI, in which it is suggested that bullying contributes to a loss of 18 million working days every year.

The survey was completed by 5,300 employees from the public, private and voluntary sectors. The findings were that 47 per cent of the respondents witnessed bullying in the last five years. One in ten (10.5 per cent) said they had been bullied within the last six months and one in four (24.4 per cent) said they had been bullied within the last five years. Over two-thirds of those who were bullied (68 per cent) said they were not the only victims at work. There is a clear link between bullying and negative management styles: those who had been bullied were more likely to have experienced autocratic and divisive styles of management than those who had not been subjected to bullying at work.

Ball (1998) of the Manufacturing Science and Finance Union (MSF) researched bullying and workplace stress and found that all groups interviewed considered stress to be increasing in their places of work. He found the greatest increase in bullying at work was in the voluntary and non-profit sector. All groups interviewed agreed that one of the major stress factors was the relationship between managers and the people they manage.

The MSF (1995) established that 42 per cent of their sample of representatives saw human relationships at work, including managerial style, to be 'most important' in determining levels of stress in the organisation.

Ball (1998) found, from his research using IPD (Institute of Personnel and Development) and MSF representatives, that both groups saw bullying at work to be a highly significant contributor to stress in the workplace.

In their research, Einarssen and Skogstad (1996) looked at bullying as something that happens over time and didn't count one-off instances:

> We define bullying as a situation where one or several individuals persistently over a period of time perceive themselves to be on the receiving end of negative actions from one or several persons, in a situation where the target of bullying has difficulty in defending him or herself against these actions. We will not refer to a one-off incident as bullying.

This means that even severe one-off instances of behaviour such as threats of, or even actual, physical violence would not be defined as bullying. In addition, the negative effects of bullying appeared to extend beyond those currently being bullied and included those who had been bullied in the past as well as those who had not personally been bullied but had witnessed bullying taking place.

Pearson (1999), in her research from the University of North Carolina, had responses from 775 people to a questionnaire on 'Workplace Incivility'. She was not looking at gross acts of aggression or violence, but concentrated on such instances as demeaning correspondence, making accusations with lack of knowledge, undermining another's credibility in front of others, being shouted at – behaviours that fall into the category of bullying. Her results are interesting in terms of the cost to the organisation in which her subjects worked. After the incidents,

- 28 per cent lost work time avoiding the instigator,
- 53 per cent lost work time worrying about the incident or future interactions,
- 37 per cent believed that their commitment to the organisation declined,
- 22 per cent decreased their effort at work,
- 10 per cent decreased the amount of time that they spent at work,
- 46 per cent contemplated changing jobs to avoid the instigator, and
- 12 per cent actually did change jobs to avoid the instigator.

This study provides broad insight, as the respondents worked in organisations employing between two and 100,000 employees from a cross-section of organisations across the United States.

Although this study has not yet been replicated in the United Kingdom, the research so far would indicate that the picture here is no less depressing, both for employees who just want to get on with their jobs and employers who want productive, contented staff.

At the 1999 TUC Women's Conference, the results of a survey regarding sexual harassment and bullying were announced. From these findings it appears that around five million workers have been bullied or are currently being bullied at work in the UK. Interestingly, 11 per cent of female and 11 per cent of male workers reported bullying directly. The collection of data was questionnaire-based and distributed primarily through union networks.

This research revealed that bullying was being perpetrated on multiple grounds. One young woman was being bullied because she was young, efficient, attractive and not interested (personally or sexually) in the male manager. As a result, she was given extra work, she had difficulties getting approval for the leave she requested and, in many ways, she was treated differently to other members of staff. The research found that many women are bullied for gender-related reasons and for one or more other 'discriminatory' reasons.

Men and women tended to respond differently to bullying, women being more likely to blame themselves and suffer emotionally. Men were less able to turn to anyone for support. Victims felt that being a union member was an advantage when it came to obtaining positive action to being bullied at work.

Rayner *et al.* (2002) concludes that adult bullying was less likely to be physical and could be divided into several categories:

- threat to professional status (e.g., belittling opinions, public professional humiliation, accusations regarding lack of effort),
- threat to personal standing (e.g., name calling, insults, intimidation, devaluing with reference to age),
- isolation (e.g., preventing access to opportunities, physical or social isolation, withholding information),
- overwork (e.g., undue pressure, impossible deadlines, unnecessary disruptions),
- destabilisation (e.g., failure to acknowledge good work, allocation of meaningless tasks, removal of responsibility, repeated reminders of blunders, setting up to fail).

The current situation

Cooper, co-author with Hoel of the UMIST 2000 study, said 'The findings in this study show that with better management training and awareness, bullying is avoidable. Workplace bullying not only damages the individual but everybody who experiences it.'

Hoel and Cooper (2000) carried out a study of 5,288 individuals from 70 organisations. They found that one in ten people (10.6 per cent) reported having been bullied within the last six months, rising to one in four (24.7 per cent) when the period was extended to the last five years. Almost 46.5 per cent witnessed bullying taking place within the last five years. It is worth noting that Hoel and Cooper (2000) used the Einarssen and Skogstad (1996) definition of bullying – i.e., to exclude one-off instances in their research.

Some of Hoel and Cooper's results were surprising in that respondents in supervisory or management positions were found to have been as likely to be bullied as those without management responsibility.

In Australia, the Queensland State Premier, Peter Beattie, set up in 2001 a government taskforce to study the reasons for bullying and develop ways to fight it. He states: 'The latest research shows workplace bullying affects one in four workers and cost industry nationally an estimated 12 billion Australian dollars last year.'

It is true that many changes have taken place inside organisations over the last ten years. In places of work across the country, partitions have been taken down and we see open-plan offices the size of football pitches; we have seen regular desk space replaced by systems of 'hot desking' or 'hotelling'. There is a move towards people using their modems to work from home. Dress codes have changed, favouring 'smart casual' over business attire. Titles have given way to first names. Few organisations still have separate manager and staff toilets or management canteens. Three-sixty-degree feedback allows people to tell their managers anonymously where they are not managing well. Employees undergo psychometric testing and they complete preference instruments to enable them to be categorised. All of this is to unify the people who work in organisations and help them to fit together as one team!

Systems of mentoring, coaching and professional development are adopted to enable staff to grow with their jobs. Money is spent on team building and away-days, incentive trips to the theatre, family days for all, weekends on cruise liners. Jargon is another way in which teams become united on a superficial level – a kind of 'in', restricted code that only the select few will understand.

Fortunes have been spent on courses such as change management. And yet, the questions we need to ask ourselves are:

- Are the changes that have been made for the better?
- Has a better workplace for employees been created?

Even with the best of intentions, none of these innovations can have any real meaning and nothing will happen to improve working conditions if the core values and attitudes of the company towards dignity in the workplace do not change.

Despite the greater general awareness of bullying at work, and the recent implementation of policies by many organisations, at a May 2002 conference Tehrani reported her research findings on the National Health Service (quoted in Crouch 2002):

- One in six nurses have been bullied at work over the past year.
- Three in five NHS staff have witnessed bullying at work over the past two years.

- 29 per cent of black and Asian nurses, and 41 per cent of nurses with a disability, have been bullied over the past year.
- 41 per cent of victims say their immediate supervisor or manager was the person responsible.
- One in ten victims show symptoms similar to post-traumatic stress disorder.
- Nurses face the highest levels of workplace bullying in occupational health, learning disabilities, nurse education and health visiting.
- 57 per cent of bullied nurses are not satisfied with the way their employers have handled the situation.
- One in three bullied nurses intends to leave the profession over the next 12 months.

These findings suggest that awareness and policy adoption have not affected all organisations equally; as far as some NHS Trusts are concerned, they appear to be at risk of not only losing valuable staff but also facing legal claims brought by them.

It seems that organisations still have a long way to go towards wiping out unacceptable behaviour. I believe the solution is about researchers, organisational personnel, health professionals, trainers, counsellors and psychologists joining forces to both understand and educate.

Leymann (1996), discussing the industrialised western world, described the workplace as the only remaining 'battlefield' where people could run into each other without being taken to court. I agree wholeheartedly with this notion and have to add that unless bullying at work is taken seriously, more and more people will be psychologically injured or worse.

The bullying culture

While some organisations are facing up to, and dealing with, bullying, others do not consider it a priority. This latter attitude is dangerous because it can lead to a bullying culture pervading the organisation. The MSF (1995) stated that:

> Bullying affects not only the individuals involved but the organisation as a whole, since people working in a climate of fear and resentment do not give their best. Where bullying

occurs and is not dealt with, sickness absence will increase, staff turnover will rise and morale and performance levels will fall. The organisation will suffer loss of production, increased sickness and retraining costs, a threat to its public image as well as the potential for further public exposure through cases taken to Industrial Tribunals.

Organisations that leave themselves open to the creation of a bullying environment usually find low levels of morale amongst employees, high rates of sickness absence and an unusually high turnover of staff. Most people who are bullied and harassed at work don't say a word; they just leave.

I often suggest to Human Resources departments that one way of assessing their own organisations is to look at the staff turnover rates. Is the turnover higher in some departments than in others? Is there a valid reason for this? Or is the determining factor a long-term manager or other member of staff who may be responsible?

An organisation's credibility in the marketplace can be damaged if its mission statement professes respect for all its employees and customers, while internally it fosters a culture that leaves people feeling unhappy, afraid and always on the lookout for alternative employment.

Wright and Smye (1997) discuss three types of abusive work cultures. First is the *win/lose culture* where everyone is out for themselves. In this type of work culture there is withholding information from colleagues, a highly competitive atmosphere and no teamwork. Second, there is the *blame culture*. Here, individuals are afraid to step out of line for fear that they will be picked on and blamed for doing something wrong. Third, there is the *sacrifice culture*, in which people put their jobs before their social and personal lives to such an extent that they eventually become ill. All three of these abuse cultures are not only bad for morale, but bad for business too.

Bullying cultures are created by the attitudes of the people responsible for running organisations. Well-designed mission statements are of no benefit to the employees if the people at the top neither notice them nor adhere to them. When an organisation says, 'There is no bullying here; we have protected ourselves against precisely that kind of behaviour because we have policies', cause for concern exists. Policies will benefit both employer and employees only if they are put into practice.

Bullying cultures are unlikely to be led by a management team that sets a good example or is conscious of the importance of being good role models. In the main, bullying is modelled from the top down, and what is seen lower down reflects what is happening above.

An autocratic leadership style of management is associated with a high incidence of bullying. The worst examples of this that I have come across are those where managers make the gestures of listening to the opinions of the team, but then undermine any ideas put forward. This is often also combined with 'micro-management' where staff members are given very little autonomy and hardly any responsibility for their work. They are also constantly monitored. I saw a gross example of this when I carried out a stress audit in a public company. In one department, the supervisor sat in an elevated glass-enclosed office, which enabled him to watch his team working below. He timed how long they spent on toilet visits and barked orders over the tannoy if he thought any of them were having an unnecessary conversation. His nickname amongst the anxious staff was 'Hitler'. When I discussed his style of management with the people in Human Resources, they in effect colluded with him when they replied, 'He's going to retire soon.' Not soon enough for many of his team, however!

The bullying culture breeds a negative atmosphere, one in which there are only criticisms and no praise for a job well done. There is no recognition of the positive contributions that people make and there are often unclear boundaries so that people do not know what is expected of them. People are anxious about taking on more work when a colleague is away in case the extra duties should remain with them and they are expected to move forward with unrealistic workloads. In a bullying culture unrealistic objectives are set and then obstructions are placed in the way to prevent the employee from achieving them.

The bullying culture thrives in an atmosphere of lies and negative rumours. One man who had been the subject of lies about a liaison with a female colleague begged me to tell his wife that it was not true. He was not part of the 'pub culture' that the managers encouraged and, frequently, those who did go drinking used to invent rumours and untruths about him 'just for a laugh'. On one occasion his wife received a phone call from a woman pretending to be his mistress. The man reached the stage where he dreaded going into work on Monday mornings only to have a 'friend' tell him the latest crop of untruths about him invented the previous Friday evening at the pub.

Some cultures collude with bullying behaviours. People talk of being hounded by the press. 'Hounding' is simply bullying by another name and is not the exclusive preserve of celebrities. The press has gained notoriety for the methods they use to gain stories from people in organisations. Working with press officers suffering from stress has given me an insight into their major stressors. Some members of the press literally harass younger press officers for information they do not have, or do not have permission to reveal. This process can continue until the young officers are stressed to the point of giving up their careers. Other organisational cultures collude with bullying behaviours by not doing anything about the way in which outside agencies treat their staff.

A bullying culture can also be created by a management that tolerates the bullying of their employees by customers. By sitting quietly in a public office, like a department of social security or the passport office, it is possible to observe gross examples of bullying. The public employees in these offices are often harassed and bullied by people who display racist, intimidating, and threatening behaviour. This often happens because, based on stereotyping and prejudice, the general public often expect them to be unhelpful and treat them accordingly. The public servant feels defensive and even afraid. In this way, an atmosphere of abuse is established.

Employers need to take note of the way in which not only the staff treats one another within the organisation but also the way customers treat them. They also need to be prepared to take the appropriate action.

Smith and Sharp (1994) in their work on school bullying describe bullying as 'the systemic abuse of power'. This is equally the case in adult bullying; bullies are usually in positions of some power – but they take more.

Sutton (2001) found that school bullies were no less bright than children who did not bully; in fact, they scored higher than many other groups on social cognition. From my experience of working with people accused of bullying, they are socially competent and often very quick, alert thinkers.

We may believe that workplace bullying has no similarity to school bullying, yet this is not true; terms like 'wet' originated in the public schools. Some organisations perpetuate the social class system, no relevance being given to a person's competence but only to the school or university they went to. Academic qualifications and a CV showing relevant experience are often ranked higher than a person's inherent skills even if the job being interviewed for is primarily a people-management role.

Lawrence (2001) suggests that many researchers have found power or power imbalance to be a key issue in bullying at work. Brodsky (1976) sees bullies manipulating their colleagues and staff to gain more power or privilege and points out that some positions of power (e.g., the Marine Corps drill instructor) can be interpreted as a justification for aggressive behaviours.

Twenty years on, Einarssen and Skogstad (1996) found an actual or perceived imbalance of power between the protagonists. They noted that power could be formal (such as in a supervisory or management role) or an informal, assumed power. Exploiting personal contacts, abusing organisational standing, plus the knowledge of a person's vulnerability are examples of the way in which people gain informal power.

Archer (1998) found that the most predominant form of bullying is isolation and exclusion. People want to be accepted into a team. They can either challenge this behaviour and run the risk of its getting worse or they can wait and hope, like children in the school playground, that the bullies will change their minds and then want to include them in their gang.

People are influenced by the culture they work in. And because they want to fit in, many start to behave in ways that they have to learn in spite of their own natural inclinations. For instance, some cruel behaviours are colluded with under the guise of 'tradition' – these include rites of initiation, which are frequently nothing more than legitimised humiliation of the juniors or apprentices. These behaviours are often dismissed as 'just a joke' and something that everyone has to go through. But they are not a joke; this is bullying.

Examples of the bullying culture

The following scenarios show the existence of a bullying culture or describe conditions in which such a culture can easily originate:

- *Performance-related pay can be used as a way of bullying people.* Employees strive to do an ever-increasing volume of work within decreasing timescales and with fewer resources.

Yet, at pay-review and appraisals time, they are told that their quality of work has deteriorated.

- *Micro-management.* Constantly monitoring and assessing employees, if taken to extremes, can be interpreted as bullying, as job satisfaction is stifled, resulting in employees feeling powerless and out of control.
- *Pressure.* Pressurising employees with unrealistic workloads under the guise of needing to 'raise performance levels' is likely to have the opposite effect by encouraging under-performance.
- *Mergers.* When two businesses combine, a bullying culture can be created when the more powerful organisation takes over, quashing both the values and the people-culture in the smaller company.
- *Reorganisations.* Employees can be treated unfairly during reorganisations. People can be made redundant when job specifications are redrafted in such a way as to render them ineligible to apply for their own jobs. Alternatively, the specifications may be changed and, even if the individual stays, they will probably fail as they cannot cope with the unrealistic demands being made of them. This leads to a demoralised person leaving the company – or the company having grounds to fire them. I refer to this as a psychological game of 'I can make you fail'. Sometimes people are redeployed in a lower status job (with their pay reduced accordingly).
- *Privately owned businesses.* In an actual case, I found that the managing director bullied anyone who came in as his second-in-command. When they eventually succumbed to the pressure, the MD made sure that he gave them a large payoff conditional upon a non-litigation clause.
- *Jargon.* The use of specific language is a way of marginalising people working within the same organisation. Jargon is often developed by the few to create a means of communicating that divides and excludes.
- *Unrealistic working hours.* Another case: a certain employee had not seen his small children awake for four days owing to being at his desk from 7 a.m. to 9 p.m. On the fourth day he was leaving at 6 p.m. (even though his contracted leaving time was 5 p.m.) and was subjected to comments such as 'Having a half day, John?' and 'Someone doesn't want his bonus . . .'

- *Deadlines.* People set timescales or sell services to clients that are totally unrealistic, leaving support staff to struggle to deliver on the promises.
- *Maintenance of tradition.* Archer (1998), in his study of the Fire Service, found that part of the cultural norm is the 'maintenance of tradition' in this classically hierarchical structure. He quotes one fire-fighter victim who admitted: 'The tradition is that this is the way everybody gets treated but everybody can't handle it in the same way. The tradition hurts a lot of guys.'

Archer found further that 28 per cent of male, and 38 per cent of female, respondents had experienced bullying. One Equal Opportunities officer stated: 'When we referred to the person as a bully the answer we got was "He gets things done."' It is believed that individuals are bullied because of their sex and race in order to perpetuate the domination of the white male culture. As a Brigade principal officer put it: 'Those are the ones I call the Iron Heads; they just don't get it and they are willing to break the rules to prove a point.' So long as this white male dominance goes unchallenged the bullying culture in this uniformed organisation will continue.

Archer reports different attitudes to the treatment of recruits in his study. One fire-fighter victim stated: 'I think it's tradition in the fire brigade that what we now class as bullying has always been teasing and it has been stuff which everybody is supposed to put up with.' As the Brigade Equal Opportunities officer stated, 'I was harassed when I started. It makes a man of you. It builds character.'

Archer concludes that the biggest contribution to bullying behaviours and the most damaging to the individual is the socialisation process that occurs when an individual joins the group. In order to be accepted they are subjected to sexual innuendo, nicknames, jokes, rumours and horseplay under the guise of team building.

- *'The right fit'.* People are recruited to work in an organisation because they possess certain wanted characteristics, which are seen to perpetuate the existing culture. One Human Resources recruiter said: 'I know they are arrogant and bullying, but these are the people they want.' This type of person can be recruited ostensibly because they are driven and will get things done. 'We only want Type A personalities here – no wimps or plodders.'

- *Power play.* Informing people that, say, within the next year 10 per cent of them will lose their jobs is certainly going to contribute to a culture based on insecurity and fear. People become anxious, they might put their lives on hold; choose not to go ahead with planned moves or holidays and generally worry because of their financial commitments. Many start to work unrealistically long hours in order to appear hard-working, loyal and indispensable, whether or not this extra time is actually warranted.

- *Specific industries and functions within them are conducive to bullying behaviour.* One magazine aimed at young models asked if I considered whether photographers' shouting at the young models and telling them to 'Smile and get your tits out darling' was bullying. When the models refused, they were subjected to abuse. Of course, this is bullying twice over. Many of these pretty teenage girls went home in tears, their dreams soured.

- *Abuse of personal affiliations.* Managers who have special relationships with the senior management team, (e.g., are golf buddies or personal friends) usually enjoy an added bonus: their questionable behaviours are ignored. We have had many examples of managers using intimidating threats of discipline by saying things like 'There is no point in complaining – I'm married to the Chairman's daughter', or 'I am *very* close friends with the Managing Director.'

- *Isolation.* Teamworking is fine so long as it works. However, teams have to be managed in such a way that those people with the loudest and strongest opinions do not override the more quiet members. People can feel shut out and isolated if they are not encouraged to participate within the team.

- *Unacceptable management style.* When those at the top of an organisation do not take their leadership role seriously – e.g., by not demonstrating listening skills, by being quick to act without thinking things through, showing insensitivity to others' feelings, making unreasonable demands – a bullying culture trickles down.

- *Inaction to complaints.* When bullying is reported, either to management or Human Resources staff, the complainants are sometimes fobbed off with 'I will have a quiet word with them.' The victim frequently believes – not without good reason – that nothing will be done to remedy the problem. By not following a set, transparent procedure, the management creates an environment in which a bullying culture thrives unchecked.

• *'You asked for it.'* Attitudes of personnel range widely. Some employees even have the attitude that people who are bullied must have asked for it, or that bullying doesn't happen to real men. The victims, aside from being bullied, also have to deal with the added burden of shame.

• *Management becomes accessory to the behaviour.* If employees approach their line managers or Human Resources about the way in which they are being treated and receive comments such as 'No one has ever complained before', 'It's just a personality clash' or, even worse, 'He is more valuable to us than you are', this reflects management's implicit collusion with inappropriate, unacceptable and unprofessional behaviour.

An alternative to a bullying culture

In an alternative culture people manage their own time and they are judged by their results (not by the number of hours they are to be seen at their desks). If they have a medical appointment they can go without an inquisition, working from home is possible and shorter working weeks are negotiable. In these days of easy remote access, none of the above should cause problems to a people-focused culture.

Wright and Smye (1997) discuss a US law firm that set limits on the number of hours that staff can work. They also have a policy of not paying their senior staff unrealistically high salaries compared to the more junior staff. This results in people wanting to work at the firm.

The support staff who keep things ticking over deserve the same respect as the professional fee earners. Think of the disruption that would be caused in a busy organisation if there was no coffee in the machines, the rubbish bins not emptied, the toilets not cleaned and the printing not done.

In an alternative culture, equal weighting is given to performance and people skills in managers' evaluations. Someone who brings in good revenues and achieves good results, but who has a transient and unhappy team under him/her, is likely to be prey to long-term disadvantages. Those managers who almost live at work and expect others to do the same have no respect for the personal lives of others. Some managers even expect their staff to keep them company in the bar, after work. This 'baby-sitting' of managers is to be discouraged.

Similarly, appraisals should not reveal any surprises. If the employee's performance had been less than satisfactory, they should be given constructive feedback on an *ongoing* basis long before the appraisal. This would ideally take the form of discussions as well as written objectives to enable the employee to put right what may have gone wrong.

When employees are under-performing, effective managers ask themselves questions such as 'What is *my* part in this; am I giving sufficiently clear instructions?' and 'Am I taking my managerial role seriously in helping this individual achieve his objectives?'

The organisation should acknowledge and understand that just because someone may be good at their job, and their appraisals are outstanding, this does not necessarily mean they are good managers or that they don't need further training. These training programmes would fill any gaps in the manager's people skills and give them an understanding of the effect of their behaviours on others. People throughout the organisation need measurable, realistic goals and objectives. They also need clear feedback throughout on how they are doing. Simply being told at the end of a year that they have not met what was expected of them is not helpful.

Well-thought-out appraisal systems must not only be a high priority, they must also be seen to be taken seriously by top management. Too often people are heard to say 'I should have had my appraisal last November and it's now July. My manager just didn't get round to it.' This is sending the psychological message to the employee that they are not important enough for their manager to spend their time on.

Bridges (1992) states that 'the first task of real organisational development is to deal with the organisational shadow' (i.e., the covert dynamics bubbling underneath the surface, the hidden agendas that are present in corporate life).

Johnson (1993) wrote a book entitled *Owning Your Own Shadow*, and Firth and Leigh (1998) talk about 'the freedom and creativity and truth and potential that lies in the corporate shadow'.

This concept of the shadow side of the organisation is not new. Rose (2001) found that although Jung was referring to the shadow of the individual self, his ideas could be translated into the organisation.

That which is hidden and not dealt with is the shadow. Failure to acknowledge that bullying exists within organisations can form part of the shadow.

Egan (1994) links the shadow with organisational culture, dealing with 'the covert, the undiscussed, the undiscussable, the unthinkable'. Significant activities and arrangements that remain unidentified and undiscussed will fall outside the reach of ordinary managerial intervention. Consequently, these matters are not tackled and will substantially affect both the productivity and quality of work life in the organisation. Egan demonstrates the significant social, financial, psychological and lost opportunity costs to organisations if shadow issues are not addressed. In an alternative culture, these issues are addressed.

In a culture of no retribution, constructive feedback can be helpful in an individual's self-development and their professional development. Here, people writing 360-degree feedback actually own and sign it. In contrast, unsigned or anonymous feedback creates the opportunity for criticism to be destructive, which can leave the recipient feeling paranoid, resentful and confused.

Unclear and vague feedback such as: 'It has been said . . .' or 'I have heard rumours that . . .' can lead to unhappy individuals and, hence, an unhappy and unproductive team. The alternative is straight, unambiguous messages that communicate what needs to be passed on. Each person in the organisation should learn to ask themselves: 'What exactly do I have to say? Is it rumour? Unkind? Destructive? Unnecessary? Do I have to say it at all?'

Employees need to feel valued, respected and appreciated in terms of appropriate core values. Examples of these core values are honesty, integrity, respect for all individuals irrespective of social status, age, sexual orientation or culture, recognition of role boundaries and accountability, openness, teamworking and team building.

Respect for colleagues can be shown in two ways. First, by open communication, i.e., *what* is said. Second, by the way people behave towards each other. It is of little value if a supervisor says appreciative words in public, but behaves differently in private. Unless the two actions are congruent, it is the negative behaviour message that is the more powerful.

Careful selection and recruitment are the keys to bringing in personnel who fit with the alternative culture that is aimed for.

And it is at the interview stage that the interviewer can find out whether the applicant respects the values that underpin the alternative culture. Are they prepared to listen as well as be listened to? Do they find the concept of dignity at work relevant or 'just the current fad'? Interviewers must be willing to challenge applicants about their CVs. Why did they leave previous places of work? What do they know about equal opportunities, diversity and fairness at work? How much value do they place on people skills? These are all areas that can be neglected when employers are short-staffed and need to find someone who can 'do the job'. The reality is that selecting someone solely on those grounds may lead to a greater cost to the whole organisation in the longer term.

It is normal for people to disagree, and it is reasonable to expect people to acknowledge their differences in an atmosphere of respect and without taking the criticism personally. The disagreement needs to be contained in a space where confidentiality is observed. This will prevent situations from escalating out of control with other employees taking sides and causing greater division.

All of the above will need to be supported by agreed systems and processes. Most of all they will need to be *adhered to* and *modelled* from the top of the organisation downwards.

The behaviours and skills required of senior staff for effectiveness in modern organisations include the ability to work productively in teams, to share decision-making in achieving common goals, and to manage the ambiguity sometimes caused by overlapping accountabilities and responsibilities (when, for example, there are dual and dotted reporting lines). It also requires senior managers to not only manage their own relationships with staff and colleagues at all levels but in addition be aware of the relationships of those people within the organisation.

Whatever the potential for organisational confusion and conflict, efforts must be focused on meeting the objectives set by the organisation and that any questions about roles, responsibilities and accountabilities are resolved in a manner that reflects respect for the dignity of all individuals.

Many people find themselves in management roles that they have difficulty in coping with or require training in. The organisation owes it to every employee – and to its own bottom line – to introduce a system of management training, sound recruitment and selection criteria, ongoing appraisals and dealing proactively with absences.

First, managers need training in listening skills, stress management, basic communication skills, and an understanding of the value of the company's mission statement and policies – especially those dealing with harassment and bullying. Second, they must be taught to lead and motivate people. Leaders need to be credible; this means giving instructions that are congruent with the way in which they behave. The manager who demands respect from his team and then shouts and screams at them is not a credible leader.

There should be mandatory awareness-raising programmes for all staff and management training where applicable. One problem with such programmes when they are non-compulsory is that it is usually only the staff members who least need them who attend! The people who say they 'can't find the time' are generally the ones who need them most. One major organisation is finding a way of linking compulsory training with the requirements for achieving the annual bonus. These training days could be particularly relevant for getting out the message on harassment and bullying and helping staff to understand the company's stand on these behaviours and how the policy works. Policies need to be frequently updated and relaunched to keep them fresh in the minds of all management personnel.

The importance of a Human Resources team that is not only committed to, but also educated in, the underlying values of an alternative culture is obvious. HR personnel with some training in listening and counselling skills will know when to refer people to the professionals who can help them. This is effective because it costs less in time, employees get what they need, and they feel listened to and valued.

For Human Resources departments with an Employee Assistance Programme in place to which they can refer employees, there is an added advantage: support for themselves when they need it.

The alternative culture practices an equal-opportunities policy and is not just using the right jargon. It seeks to remove the glass ceiling and is realistic about job sharing and short working weeks for women with small children. The alternative culture actively challenges discrimination wherever it arises and rewards employees for their people skills and not just results.

Management should keep detailed records of the numbers of grievances, disciplinary procedures, sickness absences and dismissals within each section of an organisation. This can be an indicator of what is going on within the organisation. Exit interviews can also give information about the pervading culture because people may feel safer to discuss openly what has happened to them once they have another job to go to. Sometimes people are so angry or hurt by what they have experienced that they do speak openly about it, even without a guarantee of future employment.

Employees need to feel comfortable about using an internal complaint procedure to report instances of bullying and harassment they have been subjected to, or have witnessed, without fear of personal reprisal. One way of facilitating this is by appointing named individuals throughout the organisation whom they can approach in the first instance.

In an alternative culture the more junior grades have a real voice in management, which reduces the potential for bullying and power mongering by middle management. For instance, it is very distressing when junior members of staff find out what is happening in their organisation from the news media. Many people feel that the reason they are kept in the dark is that it gives their line managers more power. One way to avoid this situation is for all levels of staff to be represented at meetings that affect them and their future. This is especially important for non-unionised organisations.

Many workers complain that though they are asked what they think, or what ideas they have, they believe from experience that their opinions don't matter. A system of communicating higher up the chain is essential. People in organisations need to feel heard in order to feel valued. An incentive or bonus system for innovative ideas has worked well in some organisations.

Hoel and Cooper (2000) suggest that organisations 'undertake regular risk assessments or stress audits to identify bullying at work'. Organisations need a core of trust. If employees do not trust each other then there is no moving forward, as no one is willing to take risks. Many of us will have lately been hearing the term 'no-blame culture'. What does this actually mean? In theory, it means that if mistakes are made they do not need to be covered up for fear of blame attaching to any individual or division. Instead, the question to be asked is 'What have I, or we as an organisation, learnt from this?' A no-blame culture allows employees to take responsibility for their own mistakes without fear, and encourages people to take risks.

Bagshaw (2000) puts forward the idea that organisations need to expand their emotional capital, seeing this as more important than their knowledge capital. Bagshaw considers emotional capital to be one of the prime outcomes of training an organisation in emotional intelligence, the key component linking 'head' and 'heart' and enabling both business relationships and business projects to improve. Without expansion in emotional capital, other change is difficult. Organisations that do not take the emotions of their workforce into account are dismissing, possibly to their detriment, a major constituent of what drives and regulates the behaviour of their human assets. By dealing with group and individual emotional life events, people are enabled to move on and not feel stuck or ashamed. Businesses that afford them this opportunity will reap the benefits in a more efficient workforce.

We have moved away from the 'jobs-for-life' culture. Organisations want people who are willing to be flexible and to meet the changing needs of business in the twenty-first century.

It is no longer the norm for organisations to take care of individuals' career paths; most organisations expect employees to manage their own careers. There are exceptions to this, such as organisations that have a 'buddy', 'parenting' or 'staff manager' system, where a more senior member of staff takes on the role of counselling, mentoring or coaching more junior members of staff.

The mentor or 'buddy' acts as a source of information, emotional support and offers suggestions for handling difficult situations. They also have a good working knowledge of the organisational culture and can help new employees acclimatise to a new working environment. They will also be familiar with the company's policies and know what to do if things go wrong.

The mentor can help create a supportive work environment conducive to a highly productive and happy working team. Often this is achieved by the mentor working as a role model.

A culture in which individuals grow and maximise their potential is one that takes both personal and professional development seriously.

The attitude of senior management should be that development is positive and that training courses add value throughout the enterprise. The days of 'We are far too busy for people to go off and navel gaze' are over. The following quote from a senior police service manager might make delightful reading, but unfortunately it also suggests poor management: 'My officers are far too stressed to have the time to attend stress management courses!'

Managing conflict and stress within organisations has never been so important. Neither has the need for careful management. The idea of the 'lean, mean organisation' implies that people who cannot cope have to go. The unfortunate and unacceptable result of this might be that some individuals who don't fit are 'bullied' out.

Employers need to look at why their staff are failing. How often, when someone leaves or is not reaching their agreed objectives, does the senior person ask themselves 'What can I do to help this person succeed?'

When an employee leaves on bad terms, how many managers ask themselves 'What was my part in this person's failure?' People who fail seldom do so with their self-esteem intact. Do we ask questions such as 'Could this have been avoided?'

If we are to create genuine no-blame cultures, we need an environment of trust and honesty. Creating such a culture gives people the opportunity to be self-aware, to take pride in their role and to self-motivate.

Ishmael (1999) refers to the alternative culture as a 'positive work environment' in which people are able work to the best of their ability while pursuing the goals of the organisation.

The following, adapted from Ishmael (1999), are the characteristics of a positive work environment:

- The culture is one in which every individual is treated well and with respect.
- The behaviour of the managers and senior members of staff provides role models to their teams.
- There is a genuine concern for people's working lives.
- Self-awareness and listening to others is encouraged.
- The company actually lives up to, and acts in accordance with, its mission statement.
- Respect is given to the work/life balance.
- People are empowered to do their jobs.
- Conflict is dealt with immediately and openly.
- Complaints of inappropriate behaviour are listened to and taken seriously.
- An atmosphere of trust and support is present at all levels with everyone working to a common purpose.
- The Human Resources department is part of the overall organisational team.
- The environment supports the free expression of diversity.

Where, in an organisation, there are gaps between what is said and what is done, cognitive dissonance develops. This leads to cynicism and low morale. People need to feel that they have some control and power over what they are doing. In order to achieve this people need to be heard. One of the most important skills a manager of people can learn is to have active dialogue with their team and to listen with empathy. It is well documented that when their emotional needs are not met, people are unlikely to work to the best of their skills and knowledge.

People learn best when they feel safe and when the child within them is free to think in a divergent way, make mistakes in exploratory meetings and not fear being made to feel foolish. In such an environment our assumptions can be challenged.

Bagshaw (2000) talks about an emotional virus in organisations, which can be negative or positive. The positive virus means that people spread an air of being positive where those around them can feel good and uplifted. A negative virus is often more infectious; people are afraid to take risks for fear of making mistakes and being put down. A challenging culture is one in which people grow from experiences instead of shrinking from them. This is what we need to encourage.

To summarise, the following list has been adapted from the work of Holland (1998) and serves as a guideline for a healthy alternative culture to one in which bullying and harassment are colluded with:

- Openness.
- Respect.
- Honesty.
- Accountability.
- Trust.
- Recognition and respect for the boundaries.
- Being allowed to get on with day-to-day matters.
- Aiming for win/win outcomes.
- More open involvement in decision-making.
- Agreeing appropriate channels of communication and sticking to them.
- Listening to others.
- No undermining.
- No blaming.
- No shaming.
- No gossip.

- No victimisation.
- No indiscreet comments.
- No 'humour' at another's expense.
- Giving due regard for confidentiality.
- No offensive written material, e.g., calendars, posters, e-mails, faxes.
- Working together to reconcile potential conflict.
- Feeling respected and treating others with respect.
- Acknowledging differences without personal agendas being involved.
- Conducting disagreements respectfully.
- More face-to-face contact.
- Taking responsibility for our own part in making it work.
- Taking responsibility for our own part in its not working to date.
- Increased comfort and confidence in exploring issues.

Counselling in organisations

According to McLeod and McLeod (2001), the provision of confidential face-to-face counselling for employees is one of the most important ways in which both the public and the private sector have delivered support to their staff over the past 20 years.

There are two main models for workplace counselling:

1 *External employee assistance programmes* (EAPs). These programmes, provided by organisations to their employees, typically consist of three-, six- or eight-session modules in which any employee and (in some contracts) members of their family can avail themselves of face-to-face counselling. These services are usually offered in addition to a 24-hour telephone counselling helpline as well as legal and financial helplines.
2 *In-house counselling services* provided by counsellors and welfare officers who are employed directly by the organisation to offer all members of staff confidential counselling. Six- or eight-session modules are typical. In addition to the counselling service, the welfare personnel can also offer financial and debt counselling.

McLeod and McLeod (2001) researched the literature to date on workplace counselling and found strong evidence to support the premise that workplace counselling has a beneficial effect on psychological symptoms and well-being and on sickness absence.

They found that those people who made use of workplace counselling typically reported high levels of psychological distress. The majority of studies found that post-counselling levels of work-related symptoms and stress returned to the 'normal' range for over 50 per cent of clients. Sickness absence rates in clients were reduced by 25 to 50 per cent.

A further benefit that McLeod and McLeod (2001) report is that the studies have demonstrated that the benefit–cost ratio for workplace counselling goes beyond mere break-even, and is in fact positive (i.e., the benefits exceed the costs) (Ahn and Karris, 1989; Alexander Consulting Group, 1990; Blaze Temple and Howat, 1997; Bray et al., 1996; Bruhnsen, 1989; Houts, 1991; Karreich et al., 1987; McCellan, 1989).

McLeod and McLeod (2001) conclude as follows:

> The only policy and practice directive that is supportable by current research is that counselling of some sort should be available to all: the evidence confirms that provision of workplace counselling is beneficial not only for individual service users, but also for the organisations which employ them.

Organisations can take care of their staff in many ways, including subsidised or free canteens, gym or sport facility membership. More and more organisations are offering employee assistance programmes (EAPs) and work–life programmes.

Employee assistance programmes

Approximately 7 per cent of the working population have access to a face-to-face counsellor. However, an established EAP provider gives the employees access to a wide range of facilities, including legal and financial information.

It is not only the employees who benefit from an EAP; Human Resources personnel and managers have somewhere to refer an employee who is in need of more professional assistance with issues than they have the skills or the time to deal with.

Human Resources personnel also have access to the EAP service whether it is to deal with personal problems or issues relating to difficult situations at work.

Aspinall (2001), in her research based on an agro-chemical manufacturing centre, found that most respondents – both employees and management – considered counselling at work to be of benefit. Further, it was found that by the organisation's taking care of the psychological health of its workforce, a chicken-and-egg scenario – in which a healthy workforce engenders a healthy organisation and vice versa – ensues.

Problems that individuals may be having directly affect them as employees and cannot be separated out. This is especially valid where health and safety-at-work issues are concerned.

An EAP referral system is invaluable when dealing with cases of bullying and harassment as the parties can be referred to different counsellors for support and help in understanding what is going on for them. The victims, their colleagues, Human Resources, the manager and the perpetrator(s) can all benefit from seeing someone 'for them'.

Although EAPs are confidential, meaning that personal information relating to individuals is not fed back to the company, there is still a feedback loop that operates. After individuals have been for their one-to-one counselling they are asked to complete a questionnaire. This information, together with the statistics of use by employees, enables the organisation to evaluate if the service is fulfilling its objectives.

Jenkins and Pollecoff (2000) suggest that although counselling services appear to be a way for organisations to demonstrate compliance with health and safety law, and to reduce staff sickness, labour turnover and overall stress levels at work, these services will be less effective if they are a 'bolt-on' addition to overall staff services. They believe that what is needed is a counselling service that is fully integrated into the wider functioning of the organisation. They consider that: 'Managers may intend that workplace counselling becomes a hedge against future litigation. However, the road to court can be paved with good intentions.'

Work–life programmes

Work–life programmes are relatively new in this country; in the USA, however, they are well established. Work–life programmes are designed to help employees balance their obligations at work and their personal responsibilities by providing them with access to a range of helplines, services and facilities.

Turner and Davies (2000) in the USA referred to work–life challenges as assistance with child care, elder care, adoption, legal and financial problems, and consumer affairs. They see both EAPs and work–life programmes as being driven primarily by companies and unions wanting efficient, cost-effective solutions to employees' personal problems.

Some of the most commonly provided services and benefits are:

- handling insurance claims and negotiating with insurance adjusters;
- company policies on parental leave following childbirth or adoption;
- health and wellness programmes (e.g., advice on healthy diet and exercise);
- academic and financial referrals;
- adoption/parenting special needs;
- consultation regarding work/life balance policies;
- advice on financial and credit problems;
- legal advice;
- pet care;
- ante-natal care;
- post-natal support;
- pre-retirement lifestyle planning;
- career counselling;
- specialist services and support for expatriates.

Speaking from a US perspective, Rick Wald, a principal and national practice leader from Mercen's Work/Life Consulting Practice in Minneapolis, thinks the percentage of employers offering integrated EAP and work–life programmes will grow dramatically each year. If the growth in EAPs analysed in UK organisations is anything to go by, it could be predicted that trends here will follow suit.

Chapter 3

Bullying at work

The concept of dignity at work

People have a right to be treated well and with respect in the workplace. Many, though, are not in this position. They wake up, often from fitful sleep, and go to work with fear and dread that this is going to be another day during which they are going to be treated badly.

My sense is that by the time you have finished reading this chapter, each one of you will recognise someone either from your past or in your present who is a bully. Although this book is about bullying in the workplace, it does of course not mean that these behaviours happen only in the workplace. Children bully each other in school playgrounds or classrooms, friends bully each other and people in close interpersonal relationships bully each other. That, however, is for another book!

The key idea to bear in mind when reading this book is that bullying is not about *intention*, it is about *impact*. In other words, it is about the effects that the behaviours of one or more people have on other people.

What is bullying?

The working definition I use for bullying is the one used by the Manufacturing Science and Finance (MSF) Union:

> Persistent, offensive, abusive, intimidating, malicious or insulting behaviour, abuse of power or unfair penal sanctions, which makes the recipient feel upset, threatened, humiliated or

vulnerable, which undermines their self-confidence and which may cause them to suffer stress.

According to the Industrial Society, 'Harassment can be defined as any improper, offensive and humiliating behaviour, practices or conduct, which may threaten a person's job security, create an intimidating and unwelcoming and stressful work environment, or cause personal offence or injury.'

People who are being bullied often do not recognise that they are being bullied. They often think that they are the only one who is constantly getting it wrong and that there is something wrong with them. They often feel ashamed and that they cannot cope. Moreover, they fear that if they tell anyone they will not be believed but seen as weak and inadequate (Erskine, 1999).

Who bullies?

Most of us are capable of bullying behaviours. Thankfully, most of us prevent ourselves from acting out in this way. How many of us can say that in certain circumstances, such as when we are in a hurry and the person behind the counter is being slow or incompetent, we haven't wanted to say something rude or sarcastic? How many of us have not felt frustrated at a colleague's mistake that causes us a lot of extra work? How many times have we really wanted to say something but, instead, kept quiet. It is not bullying to feel frustrated, angry or upset at another person's behaviour; but it is bullying behaviour when we act on our feelings in an inappropriate way.

The self-righteous bully is someone who cannot accept that they could possibly be in the wrong. They are totally devoid of self-awareness and neither know nor care about the impact of their behaviour on others. These are people professional development coaches have difficulty working with to effect behaviour change. They are always right and others are always wrong. One woman whom I worked with refused to accept any responsibility for the effect that her behaviour was having on others; she wrote them off as wimps unable to take fair criticism. Another said she could work with these people again as she did not 'bear grudges'. Yet another said, 'Of course I didn't bully him. I merely said that his dress was disappointing and pointed out that depression was no excuse for his poor work performance.'

It would be incorrect to think that bullying takes place only downwards in the hierarchy. There are many examples of bullying by junior members of a team. For example, many lecturers have complained of harassment and bullying by their students. 'If you know what is good for you, you will rethink the grade you gave me for my last assignment. My father has known the Chancellor for years and pays for one of the college trophies.'

Another example was that of an organisation in which it appeared that the whole office was living in fear of upsetting the receptionist who had worked there longer than anyone else. She acted as unofficial timekeeper, making notes of hours worked, sickness absences and holidays even though this was not part of her job. Her own attendance and holiday details were of course ex-directory.

Bullying is not necessarily an act of one person against other. A team of people can bully one or two individuals, for instance where a team resents a former colleague's promotion or where a new manager comes in and wants to make changes. One freelance female computer programmer was brought in to manage a team of men. They would not accept instructions from her and made constant personal remarks about her – all within her hearing. This bullying caused her to leave, especially as she felt the company would not be interested in dealing with it because she was 'only' a contractor.

When teams of people get together to bully a new manager, the underlying reason can be that one member of the team, who is the psychological leader, wants the manager's job and encourages the rest of the team to support them in their inappropriate behaviours. In these cases, members of the team support out of fear rather than loyalty.

One of the most common themes of bullying behaviour can be observed when someone in a management position bullies their second-in-command. They do things such as arrange important meetings in the employee's absence and then blame them for missing agenda items or for non-attendance. I have come across this many times, especially after a manager gets back from vacation to find that his job has been done perfectly in his absence. Adams (1992) describes this as work envy, when someone in a more junior position can do their job as well as, or even better than, they themselves can do it.

People with some power who take more are usually the people who bully others. Teachers can bully children, as can other adults who are in a position of power, as we saw in the example of young teenage models who were bullied by photographers (Chapter 2).

Sometimes, when sexual relationships creep in, the balance of power can change and people become bullies. An example of this was the secretary who became the mistress of the chairman of the company and suddenly started to bully colleagues who had been her friends.

Bullying seems not to be associated with gender. Field (2001) found the split between men and women who bully roughly 50/50.

The bully

In my experience there are two main types of bully. The first type is the self-righteous bully who comes from an 'I'm OK – You're Not OK' position. These people are vulnerable to the criticism of others, have low self-esteem and project this feeling of inadequacy onto other people. Their behaviour is destructive to others and they appear to take great pleasure in seeing their victims suffer from being afraid of them. Organisations have a duty of care to protect their staff from these people.

The other main kind of bully is someone who functions from an 'I'm Not OK – You're OK' position. These people are afraid, vulnerable and behave in an inappropriate way in an attempt to protect themselves from what they perceive as danger. As a result, these bullies see themselves as victims and actually feel that it is they who are being persecuted. They don't trust people and are actually scared of being found out for their inadequacies. These people need training. They are easier to deal with and are usually willing to take feedback in the form of coaching.

A third type is the person who behaves in the way that they believe is expected, or are told is expected, of them. They may be demonstrating behaviours that the previous managers modelled or they may have had their own job security threatened in the past for being 'too soft' on their team. This is another group for whom coaching works well, and they can be trained in more appropriate ways of managing and behaving.

Although an exact profile of a bully cannot be drawn, certain characteristics set them apart. For example, bullies tell lies, over both trivial and important matters; they will give instructions and then either 'forget' what they have said or deliberately make the other person feel that they are in the wrong. Another form of lying is the withholding of information or the giving of misinformation so that others end up doing vast amounts of work as a result. The bully can then accuse the member of staff of 'getting it wrong'.

Bullies have favourites – 'flavours of the month'. In the bully's eyes, the favoured person can do no wrong and the bully places them on a pedestal, elevating them above everyone else. This can make the rest of the team resentful, especially as they tend to be blamed for any mistakes that the favourite might make. The situation can shift as quickly as it began when, suddenly, the bully's 'pet' is replaced by someone else. This fall from grace can be followed by vicious nit-picking by the bully until the pet leaves, confused and unpopular through little fault of their own. Many people have said that they are afraid of ever becoming the pet, as it usually means the next stage is to be the victim. This thought can be so unbearable that people prefer to leave the company.

Bullies have their special victims. They frequently pick on a member of the team who is not likely to answer back but is likely to blame themselves and not want to make a fuss by complaining. Other members of the team watch these behaviours going on and do not say anything for fear of being the next victim. Some people are more vulnerable to being a victim of bullying: often the immediate assistants who are contractually obliged to work with the bully. Part-time workers or juniors often feel especially defenceless and, because they have less recourse to action, don't say anything. People with mental or physical health problems and anyone from an ethnic minority background are also vulnerable. The bully has a habit of finding out from people what their weaknesses are and then using this information as ammunition. The victim invariably feels confused and they say 'I don't understand it, she was so nice to me at first – really warm and friendly.'

Typical observable behaviour from bullies is shouting, screaming and general loss of control followed, in a matter of minutes, by behaving as though nothing untoward had happened. One woman calls her staff into her office one at a time and yells at them. The rest of the team sit outside at their desks in fear of who will be next. After venting her anger she emerges from behind her desk, is sugary sweet and behaves in a coquettish way with the men.

Bullies can also use threatening behaviours, either by threatening someone physically ('Make sure you don't leave this place alone or someone will be waiting for you') or in terms of blackmail ('What would your wife say if she knew about your "friendship" with X?').

One female manager told her staff that if they did not go to an optional social event it would be reflected in their appraisal.

Bullies can take the praise for ideas or work that is not theirs and claim the resulting credit. An example of this was apparent when a junior member of the team made suggestions at an office meeting only to be ignored or pooh-poohed. Later, the bully went on to use these ideas as if they had been his own.

One research student worked very hard under the supervision of her professor. The professor wanted to put his name to a paper they were writing 'together'. She wrote the paper and he did minor alterations. She was shocked to see her name in the esteemed professional journal placed second to that of the professor. The same student was further horrified to learn that a colleague in Europe had attended a conference in which the professor had presented her research findings as his own without her consent or knowledge.

Bullies like to bring in their own team and frequently want to weed out anyone that they personally did not employ. The established staff are excluded from social events, kept out of information loops or, in some cases, actually told 'There is no longer any room for you here and it would be in your own interest to look for another job.'

Bullies generally have two very distinct sides. Cruel and calculating in the office, they are also entertaining company and great fun to be around at social occasions. Frequently in my work with victims they have said to me 'He's not always like this and is so nice after hours when we go out socially.' One set of behaviours doesn't outweigh the other; it just serves to confuse people.

It is precisely because bullies are good socially that people say, 'It must be me if everyone else gets on OK with them.' I answer this by reminding them that just because they are good fun at the pub does not mean that they are not bullies in the office. Bullies can surprise people and show some positive qualities. As one person accused of bullying said to me, 'I always send people cards if they are off sick.' Another bully said, 'I don't know what these complaints are about. I always buy them Christmas presents and take them out to lunch. We are all mates, they don't take any notice of my style.'

Bullies have been known to take formal action against their victim (saying that they are the party being bullied) if they realise that they may have gone too far and fear a complaint may be imminent. In some instances this has happened after the formal complaint from the victim has been lodged.

If challenged, bullies pretend to listen to, but not actually accept, any criticism about themselves. They will present the case of always being right and never accepting responsibility for anything that goes wrong. Instead, they blame others in an undermining way.

Bullies want to be in control at all costs. 'We haven't got time to discuss this – just get it done *my* way . . .' For victims, there is the realistic fear that any criticism they make of the bullying behaviour will be further retaliated against.

Bullies demean, devalue, misrepresent and lie to the people they work with or who work for them. They are rigid, unwilling to bend or listen to the points of view of other people. Even if they ask for ideas from their team, they are resistant to change unless they are the instigators of it.

Bullies are often intelligent people who are clever at manipulating and misrepresenting facts. They can twist what people say and confuse them until they are too upset to even try and stand up for themselves. They are not good role models, they tend to be the first to criticise the behaviours of others, even while they are guilty of the same misconduct.

Bullies 'rubbish' their staff to other people: 'I have a real bunch of stupid ****s in my team.' No wonder we don't make sales targets with that load of useless ****s – they haven't a clue.'

Bullies tend not to encourage discussion and are more likely to adopt a dictatorial approach. One man, who was the sole owner of his empire, went round the staff desks and destroyed any bits of paper that had anything personal written on them, such as a telephone number for the dentist. When challenged, he said it was his right as he owned the paper and no one was allowed to even think about their life outside of the company when he was paying their wages.

People who bully often invite themselves to meetings or conferences outside of their area of responsibility. Their colleagues are usually too scared to actually challenge them – particularly if the bully holds a senior position in the organisation. Another favourite tactic is to take over the running of the meeting and change the agenda to suit their purposes – or even to announce that they think the meeting is a waste of time, and then leave, causing everyone else present to feel deflated, incompetent and upset.

Bullies humiliate their employees. The Trade Union Congress (TUC) (1998) quotes an example: 'My ex-boss used to manage his staff by humiliation. He would make people, who did not reach the impossible targets he set, stand in the corner wearing a dunce's hat. The worst thing was he was convinced his behaviour made him a good boss and that it would increase productivity. But the staff were terrified – some of them literally jumped every time he walked in the room.'

Bullies pick on the shy and vulnerable. One woman returned from sick leave after undergoing treatment for cancer to find her chair had been swapped for a rickety old one, her desk had been moved into a dark corner away from the window and her personal things removed. She also found that a new manager had instigated these changes and he made it clear to her that there was no longer room for anyone of her age, and with her health record, in his new department.

Parody can be a subtle form of bullying. It can be so common-place that its inappropriateness is not fully acknowledged. One large team of public-sector Asian women workers were constantly upset when their colleagues mimicked their accents over the telephone. What the women found even more difficult to understand was why these people, who lived in the far north of the country, were mimicking them when they had their own very distinctive accents.

Bullies frequently behave like children. They can be snide, spiteful and vindictive when they do not get their own way. They have temper tantrums, stamp their feet and throw things around. An example of this is a picture-framer who, whenever he loses something, turns and makes nasty comments to his assistant. On one occasion he threatened to splash her with paint when he could not remember where he had put his phone. On another occasion he threatened to hit her with the broom because she had not swept the front of the shop.

Adams (1992) talks about bullies suffering from envy. In this context she means work envy, where the bully fears that a colleague could do their job as well as, or even better. Typically, in cases where they feel threatened, because the bully has some power they can resort to official actions such as unfair appraisals. Or, because they outrank their colleagues, they can cut across or ignore them at meetings, steal their ideas or – as in one example told to me – simply interrupt a colleague's presentation and take over.

These actions, together with constant criticism and never any praise (even when tight deadlines are met) are a source of deliberate bullying designed to demotivate and wear down the target individuals.

However, we see not only work envy, but also cases of personal envy. For example, a client of mine became the new 'victim' of his female boss as soon as she found out that he was getting married. She had frequently made passes at him at social functions. Another female client became the victim of bullying from her female boss at just the same time that she lost weight, started going to the gym and began to feel good and confident about herself.

Bullies make people under-perform. The way to improve performance is not to bully them, since this is going to make the situation worse. Constant nit-picking and over-monitoring of an individual's work can make their performance deteriorate and their anxiety increase. One manager who was famed in his department for constant carping told one employee, in a public office for all to hear, 'I think I should bring my 11-year-old daughter in to check your work.'

Over-supervision and meticulous checking of minutiae and details leave the member of staff feeling inadequate and powerless. Some bullies are unable to look at anything written by someone else, no matter how simple, without feeling the need to make corrections and comments. Usually the return of corrected work will be left until ten minutes before the end of the day or late on Friday afternoons.

Bullying managers often change their own revisions on a second draft back to how the employee had worded it originally. One manager beamed at a secretary as he asked for the ninth revision of a simple document late one afternoon, saying 'It will make it sexier if you do it this way . . .'

Bullying behaviours

Bullying behaviours are rarely isolated incidents. Furthermore, the first incident usually signals the beginning of a soon-to-be-established pattern. While single incidents may be seen as too subtle to be considered bullying, added together and viewed as a series, the pattern emerges.

Galen (1991) reports on an IBM employee who was forced to take early retirement or tarnish an unblemished career with an unsatisfactory job rating. The court found that he had indeed been forced out of his job and decided in his favour. He was awarded a sizeable settlement.

Assigning someone a task for which they have no training or experience can be a way of bullying them out of their job. A similar technique I have seen used is the one of giving workers 'tests' (without any prior warning) on parts of the job in which they have neither experience nor training. The bully is then able to 'prove' that the staff member is not capable of doing the job and this becomes the justification for 'letting them go'. There have been some cases of friends of the bullying manager being employed in their place.

Just as there is bullying of people to make them go, so there is also bullying them to stay. Not allowing employees to move departments, giving unfair verbal references and blocking the way for them to move within the company are ways in which a bully can achieve this objective. Frequently this occurs because it would be inconvenient to the bully to lose that member of staff. The bully has no regard to the ambitions or job satisfaction of the employee concerned.

There are two types of bullying behaviours: gross and obvious or a more subtle variety.

Gross behaviours

First I will give you examples of gross behaviours; in fact, I could write an entire book describing behaviour so bad that the reader might be forgiven for thinking it the basis for a fictitious horror movie.

Undermining behaviour

A new managing director took over the overall running of a charity. In position as the office manager was a highly competent, popular and efficient middle-aged woman. From day one he decided that he no longer wanted her or anyone to answer the telephone using their own names, only 'Mr X's office'. He listened in to all conversations and criticised any gesture of warmth or pleasantries. The office manager was no longer to sign letters in her own name, order stationery or buy anything out of petty cash without his consent. He constantly undermined any authority she previously held, he was rude to her publicly and, privately, asked her when she was leaving, since he could find someone better and cheaper. He managed to reduce all of the team to tears at various times and eventually succeeded with the office manager. Clearly delighted with himself, he said, 'Oh good! I was wondering how long this would take.'

This woman, like many others in her situation, eventually felt that she really was no longer competent and began to believe that she was making many errors where before she had run the office smoothly and efficiently. When she finally went off sick, the managing director asked her colleagues if she had any family- or age-related problems.

Changing deadlines

I have frequently been given examples of a manager insisting that a piece of work be completed by an unrealistic date. The individual or team has had to work weekends and late into the night only to find that on the appointed date the manager is not there, has taken the day off, or says they haven't the time to read it until the following week.

Using personal information

The senior member of a team publicly said to another, more junior woman, 'No wonder your boyfriend left you when you dress like that.' In another example of using personal information, a senior manager said to a woman, 'It was only fair we promoted a man; after all, your husband earns a good salary and you don't need the money.' On another occasion a male manager said to a senior female member of staff whom he had been bullying for some time: 'I hear that your husband has retired. Don't you want to retire and spend more time with him?' She felt angry and humiliated in front of her staff and colleagues.

Probably the most vindictive example of using personal information was the woman who said to her male assistant, 'Your baby being born with a disability is an act of God. It is punishment for your having had affairs.'

Being frozen out

One woman had her work taken away from her and the rest of the team was instructed not to speak to her. Being isolated is a powerful way in which people can be bullied. As social animals, we have a need to feel that we belong; not being invited to a social occasion, or even to lunch when everyone else in the office has been, can leave people feeling stressed, uncomfortable and isolated.

Abusive behaviour

Bullies can show great creativity in their use of techniques. I heard an example of this when a highly experienced secretary came into my office and asked me to listen to a tape from her dictation machine. What I heard was her male boss, a man well respected in his profession, screaming insults at her and barking instructions between telling her how stupid she is.

If we actually think about it, this example is a form of torture; the audio headphones go directly into the person's ears and there is no escape. One of the boss's favourite taunts was: 'Who else would employ you at your age?' He had picked on this woman's weakness, as there was a grain of truth in what he said. It is difficult for women in their late fifties to find employment. However, it does give me great pleasure to be able to write that this woman was headhunted by a competitor company and that she remains in that position, working happily in a community where she is appreciated and respected.

Bullying rarely ends with overt public remarks or outbursts. The worst bullying usually goes on behind closed doors and without witnesses. I have many examples of men and women bullies behaving at their worst after most of the people in the office have gone home. An example of this was a female boss who called a junior male member of the team into her office just as he was leaving the office with his colleagues. He went in and sat down, as he was requested to do. She locked the door and stood next to it, which increased his feelings of vulnerability and, knowing that he was unable to escape, yelled and screamed insults at him about being a member of her team, as a human being and, lastly, as a man.

I consider that suggesting to someone that they should seek alternative employment is a bullying behaviour. This can include remarks such as 'Wouldn't you be happier with a job nearer to home?' and 'I could easily replace you with someone younger, more efficient and cheaper' or, in one reported case, 'a trained chimpanzee'.

Sarcasm

Sarcasm is a bullying technique which is often masked by remarks such as 'People round here are too sensitive.' For example, a person goes into their office not feeling at their best and returning too early after being off sick. They find a scribbled note on the sickness absence book next to her name saying 'Taking the p**s' and someone in the office saying 'You're looking good, been on holiday?'

One woman's treatment was described in Greenhalgh's (1999) newspaper article. Her bullying manager e-mailed other staff members, citing her victim as an example of how not to do things.

So-called humour

People can be bullied in many ways under the guise of 'humour'. Jokes distributed by e-mail, cartoons on notice boards or unsuitable literature sent to people's homes are some examples. An even more extreme case was that of a funeral wreath being delivered to a person's home with their name on it.

Practical jokes or inappropriate humour cannot be passed off as 'all in good fun; we were only having a laugh' or 'It's him – he can't take a joke.' Humour at someone else's expense is not funny – it's bullying. In this category I include the initiation ceremonies that some cultures collude with. These are practical jokes or pranks carried out on junior or new members of staff. Examples of this can range from sending someone to another department for 'a long wait' to young men being 'debagged' (their trousers removed) by a group of laughing and howling women. These behaviours are bullying and can leave the victim feeling distressed and humiliated. In one bank a very senior bank clerk thought it was amusing to stamp 'turnover' on the bare legs of junior female members of staff and encouraged the junior male employees to join in the 'frivolity'. Offensive songs, graffiti and cartoons would also come under this category of bullying.

Ostensible accidents

'Accidents' can also be a thinly veiled excuse for bullying – e.g., bumping into someone carrying a cup of coffee or a tray in the canteen so that they drop or spill it and end up feeling foolish. This kind of behaviour is more likely to occur in front of an audience of other members of the team who are involved in the inappropriate treatment of another. On another occasion, one cleaning crew left a cloth that had been saturated with a toxic substance for the next shift of cleaners to move. This was the last of a long line of incidents in which a particular woman had been hurt in 'accidents' orchestrated by her management and colleagues.

Electronic harassment

The age of technology that has made communication easier has also made it easier to bully and harass people. It seems to be a common misconception that e-mail communications do not have the same value (or effect) as a letter or memo. I have been shown many examples of inappropriate and even abusive e-mail.

One such inappropriate use of e-mail was by a very senior male member in charge of a team of women who sent New Year's greetings to his staff and finished it by saying that his New Year's resolution was 'to get on with the work and stop staring at the tits of the blondes'. This man was so senior that his staff felt a complaint from them would only be used against them.

Voice mails and text messages can also be used in a similar way to bully and harass people. This can include the targeting of staff members who live alone to find threatening and anonymous messages, or heavy breathing, on their telephone-answering machines.

Sexual harassment

Sexual harassment by e-mail has become popular. One woman had nearly two hundred e-mails from the same man when she went to her desk one Monday morning. They all related to asking her out and making personal remarks about her body and her status.

Harassment under the guise of love has been brought to my attention on several occasions in the last year. Both men and women become involved with someone they work with. It usually starts as a friendship – until one falls in love with the other, who then feels harassed by the constant attention. Constant unwanted attention, particularly when the person responsible insists that it is out of concern, is still harassment.

I was asked to advise on a case of harassment through gifts. A junior receptionist received a dozen red roses on the hour, every hour, from a colleague with whom she had declined an invitation to dinner.

Invasive behaviour

Invading a person's personal space and possessions is bullying. This can include standing too close to them when it is obvious they are not comfortable, standing while they are sitting, yelling at them and going into other people's lockers, desks or bags and interfering with the contents. I have had examples of people finding out the computer passwords of their victims and going into their computers and deleting entire files – difficult to prove.

Some bullying behaviours are so extreme that the people on the receiving end are so deeply shocked that they do not expect to be believed. Two high-powered professional women, obviously rivals, encountered each other in a corridor. Ms A turned to Ms B and threatened that if she (Ms B) were to apply for a particular promotion, she would have her 'to answer to'.

Discrediting professional reputation

Casting aspersions on someone's professionalism can also be a bullying tactic, especially in the care professions where it is often used to encourage people to work unrealistic hours, well beyond the call of duty or what should reasonably be expected from them. For example, 'If you cared about your patients you wouldn't hesitate to work additional shifts.'

More subtle behaviours

The subtler forms of bullying are by their nature more ambiguous. Here, especially, a single incident is difficult to characterise as a definite bullying behaviour and, often, a few incidents taken together indicate a pattern suggestive of bullying.

Bogus scheduling

Arranging meetings and leaving a certain person off the invitation list, only to complain at the meeting 'I see that X hasn't bothered to attend', is one example.

Others such as setting unrealistic deadlines, turning down someone's request for leave or cancelling their leave at the last minute without good reason, removing responsibility from someone without grounds, ignoring them or speaking to them only through a third party or by e-mail – even if they sit on opposite sides of the room – fall into this category.

Holiday rotas, work rotas and overtime rotas can be used to bully and manipulate people. Insisting that people cancel their pre-booked holidays and weekends away when there is not a crisis are further examples of bullying. So is giving the same person all the unsociable shift hours while everyone else on the team gets the more sought-after slots.

Another example consists of refusing to allow some members of a team to attend training courses on the grounds of their being too busy when other members of the team have attended them.

Making sure that work is given to an individual at a specific time when it is common knowledge that that person leaves on time on a particular day to attend to an outside activity is a definite, albeit subtle, way of bullying a subordinate.

Hiding abuse behind company policy

Assessments, appraisals, annual reviews can also be used as instruments to bully people. People work very hard to reach deadlines, only to find they have been changed. People who actually deserve to get a pay rise are passed over whilst the 'favourites' who haven't actually reached their targets are awarded them.

Another instance of cruel, abusive treatment by a bullying manager is to choose a Friday afternoon, or the late afternoon before someone is due to go on holiday, to give them negative feedback about their work or say 'I'm not happy with your performance, but we will discuss it when you return from leave.'

Evasiveness

Bullies often abuse their colleagues by not taking the responsibility for something that is officially in their remit. 'I'm sorry you are inconvenienced. I did tell my staff to do such and such', when they clearly did not.

Some bullies have a tendency not to make eye contact, but when they do it can be in the form of a direct stare. They often make notes when they are being spoken to, instead of engaging with the person.

Controlling behaviours

A potent example of this was a meeting between the harassment investigator and the Managing Director of the organisation he was carrying out the investigation for. He was told: 'I'm sure you are not going to find anything untoward here. Did you hear what I said? I'm sure you won't find anything.' This left the investigator in no doubt as to whom one of the role models for bullying behaviour was.

Inconsistency in behaviour

People change their behaviour not only from time to time but also with different people. The manager who is shouting at someone in their office for some minor misdemeanour suddenly becomes kind and avuncular when the young secretary appears, only to return to their previously foul and inappropriate behaviour as soon as she leaves.

No thanks or recognition

Work or tasks that have been done well during a manager's absence are not commented on. Instead, looking for the smallest detail with which to find fault, the manager then complains how 'things don't run smoothly when I am away'.

Undermining someone's authority

One supervisor gave her team instructions not to take notice of the requests made by their line manager but to come directly to her instead. The team is obviously placed in an untenable position.

Demeaning behaviour

Inappropriate remarks in front of staff or customers can range from a one-off 'put down', such as 'If you paid attention to detail you would know the answer to that', through to complete character assassinations. In one instance a woman was criticised for her appearance, on the supposed fact that no one in the office liked her and on the basis that she was thought to be an incompetent mother. This was all said in front of the team that she was supposed to manage.

Rumour mongering

Some work cultures are such that spreading rumours is the norm and seen by most as being a joke. However, jokes go too far and they hurt some people. In-jokes about fictitious relationships made in front of partners can lead to disharmony at home, no matter how far from the truth they are.

In one case the rumours were so far-fetched that the victim had to ask his counsellor what they meant as he had absolutely no idea what he was being accused of. Rumours are not necessarily about an individual; they can be about friends or members of their family.

Myths and misconceptions about bullying and harassment at work

- It's in people's imaginations.
- It's another excuse for a policy.
- Policies will give people opportunities for personal vendettas and enable them to make personal complaints.
- It's the trendy topic.
- People who are bullied must have asked for it.
- It will open the floodgates for malicious complaints.
- All this PC stuff will make the workplace humourless and boring.
- People can't take a joke.
- They don't know what bullying is: When I was a child . . .
- It doesn't happen to men.
- Only men bully.
- It happens only to weak people.

- That's the way things are.
- Sexual harassment? Yes please! (Remember that people frequently use humour to mask what they feel uncomfortable about.)

Chapter 4

The victims of bullying

Who is vulnerable?

There are groups of people who are more vulnerable in their places of work than others. Recent times have brought a trend towards employing people on short-term contracts. This makes them particularly vulnerable to being bullied, as they want their contract renewed, especially if it is the bully who makes the decision. Low-status employees such as apprentices and juniors are also particularly vulnerable, as often they are too afraid of losing their job to say anything. Besides, they feel 'who is going to take my word against a senior bloke like him?'

People can be bullied through socialisation. One young Asian woman who worked as an accounting clerk was bullied by her manager, who was an older Asian man, over a period of years. The bullying was bought to the attention of senior management, but not by the woman herself. When asked why she had never complained she said 'In my culture I can't show disrespect for an older Asian man.'

People with obvious mental and physical disabilities, or who suffer from mental or physical health problems, are vulnerable to being bullied. A June 2001 survey commissioned by MENCAP, the Royal Society for Mentally Handicapped Children and Adults, indicated that nine out of ten disability sufferers had suffered bullying in the last year.

Read and Baker (1996) quoted the research designed by MIND, the mental health charity, and give the following figures. Of the 778 people questioned, 34 per cent said they had been dismissed or forced to resign from jobs; 69 per cent had been put off applying for jobs for fear of unfair treatment. 'The most intolerant sector appeared to be the health and caring sector, with some of the worst cases of unfair discrimination in nursing and social work.' Most extracts of case histories published in the report dealt with sufferers from depression. Forty-five per cent of respondents also believed that discrimination had been on the increase in the last five years.

People who choose not to join a union in a highly unionised setting, or those who choose not to take part in industrial action when many of their colleagues go on strike, are also vulnerable to bullying.

Anyone who is in a minority in their place of work is vulnerable. A woman manager in charge of a team of men had a particularly hard time, with constant comments about her hormones and the state of her love life. It is hard to imagine that comments such as these would have been made to a male manager.

One lone Muslim man working with a team of western women was constantly being jibed about going off to pray in his lunch hour. He also had to suffer being teased with food during his time of fasting.

Apprentices or juniors are vulnerable. They are frequently the only junior members of staff and because of their inexperience and naivety they are cruelly teased under the guise of humour and are expected to put up with it, just as juniors before them had to.

In some work cultures apprentices and juniors are subjected to humiliating initiation rites. This is not humour; neither is it welcoming someone to be part of the team. It is bullying.

Garrett (1997) considers that trainees are vulnerable to being bullied by the trainers because of the inherent imbalance of power. She found that in any relationship where there are role conflicts, there is potential for bullying. For example, many supervisors and trainers have the power to assess whether trainees can continue with their training. Moreover, inappropriate behaviours of trainers towards their trainees is modelling unacceptable behaviours. Older people can also be highly exposed to the risk of being bullied. One 58-year-old woman working in an office was frequently shouted at by her manager, who always ended his tirade with the question 'Who else would employ you?'

Consider that the following are all targets of bullies:

- those of a different religion, gender or sexual orientation;
- people who are shy or quiet;

- those with poor mental or physical health;
- ex-offenders;
- people with noticeable physical characteristics such as a particular colour of hair or a prominent nose;
- staff who choose not to be a member of a trade union;
- physically attractive men and women;
- older employees;
- younger employees;
- those who are particularly bright and intelligent, or those who are not.

This doesn't leave very many people out! The reality is that anyone is vulnerable, even the very sharp and aware can be caught off guard by highly manipulative, clever and often subtle bullies.

For some victims, being bullied at work plays directly into their belief system about themselves. In Transactional Analysis terms, these would be called 'script beliefs'. For example, a child who is constantly put down and criticised in her family will not be surprised at being treated in a similar way by her colleagues or line manager when she grows up. She firmly believes that there is 'something wrong' with her and, therefore, is responsible for what is happening to her.

Many highly competent and professional people are afraid to admit to anyone outside or, in some cases, even to themselves, that they are being bullied. Instead, they think 'I should be able to deal with this.' Mead (2001) discusses in his press release the vulnerability of black and Asian doctors: 'Discrimination begins in medical schools and affects the person's whole career. Harassment and bullying from both colleagues and patients are daily facts of life for black and Asian doctors.'

People frequently do not report bullying because they are embarrassed and afraid that it will escalate; they are afraid that it may be 'their fault' or they fear getting the perpetrator into trouble. Most people don't want this outcome; they just want the behaviour to stop.

People may be afraid that if they make a complaint their friends and colleagues will reject them. As one woman put it, 'No one likes a grass.' In one incident, a woman who was being sexually harassed was criticised by her female colleagues when she made a formal complaint. She was told 'Why are you doing this to him? He could lose his job.'

Other reasons that people may put up with bullying behaviour include:

- Prestige of working for an organisation.
- Fear of the unknown.
- Fear that others will find out that there is something wrong with them.
- The position will look good on the CV.
- Too many job changes will look bad on the CV.
- Fear of telling potential employers why they left a previous job.
- Fear of 'exposure' to family and friends.
- Fear of upsetting family and friends.
- Fear of retaliation by family and friends.
- They have lost their confidence and are scared of the interview process.

People need to recognise when are being treated inappropriately. Their next step is to acknowledge that they do not deserve such treatment. When people think that this is just the way they are, and nothing will change, they take on a harmful 'shut up and put up with it' attitude.

People sometimes tolerate being bullied because they do not know who to complain to, they have never heard of a company policy to deal with their situation, and they are afraid that they won't be believed or taken seriously. It is up to the organisation to make all members of their staff know how to recognise bullying and give them directions as to who will help them deal with it. It needs to be made clear to all staff that not all procedures are formal and that they can seek informal help.

People who are being bullied might believe that they have left it too late and that they now have to live with it.

In some cases people feel trapped; they don't want to leave their job or move to another department for a number of reasons and they are afraid that if they say anything there will be some form of reprisal. This fear is often justified.

Crawford (1998) refers to these people giving up, 'feeling so demoralised that they cannot be bothered to fight', and he sees this as playing directly into the tyrant's hands. Once the bully or tyrant has destroyed the individual's confidence, they can do what they like with them.

Who suffers?

The direct victims, those on the receiving end of bullying behaviour, are not the only ones who suffer. In this section, unless accredited to another author, all the examples I have used are cases that I have personally come across or worked with. For confidentiality, identifying details have been changed or disguised.

Victims. People will say things like 'I have been an engineer for 20 years and I served in the army; I should be able to handle this young woman who has been given a management role over me.' This macho concept of men who should be able to handle anything is one that I come across time after time. 'I'm a man, I should be able to deal with this, I have never been weak before. Perhaps I'm not the man I thought I was.'

Family and friends. The person who is being directly bullied may be one victim but there may be many hidden victims. A person is unlikely to be able to keep their distress from their immediate family, even if they don't actually verbalise it. Partners may wonder what they have done to contribute to the distress. Children cannot understand why the ground rules at home have suddenly changed: behaviour that was acceptable previously is now considered to be too noisy or too demanding. Friends can feel shut out if not told what is going on or cannot understand what they have done to offend their previously fun and jovial friend. Friends can also feel helpless at being unable to do anything to help. Advice, when offered, may be ignored or seen as impossible to take. Members of the extended family can become involved when they become aware that something is wrong.

Colleagues. People who witness incidents of bullying at work may feel both powerless and guilty – guilty that they do not stand up for their colleague for fear of becoming the next victim. Instead they say nothing and suffer stress. People have told me about events that they witnessed years ago and about which they are still feeling bad because they did not do anything at the time. Hoel and Cooper (2000) found that 47 per cent (almost half) of Britain's employees had witnessed bullying in the workplace in the last six months.

Managers. When inappropriate behaviours are going on amongst their team members, managers can feel the stress. Many have been accused of burying their heads in the sand and many have actually agreed with this, admitting that they hoped the problem would just go away without their having to deal with it.

Personnel departments. Human Resources staff can feel very stressed and wish they could find excuses for bullying behaviours, such as 'It must be a personality clash', or 'It can't be going on here, she is such a nice woman'. One of the major difficulties for these people is that they often have to listen to stories of bullying and unacceptable behaviours about their own bosses and someone much more senior than themselves. They themselves may also have their own job-security issues or fear also becoming a victim.

Even the bullies themselves. Those people who bully through ignorance suffer when they are made aware of their behaviours. One woman said: 'I'm devastated that I have caused people so much pain, I always thought I was a good manager; my father taught me how to handle people to get a good job done.' Sadly, her father's generation had a far different attitude to management – his carrot-and-stick approach to running a department is no longer acceptable.

Another man was mortified when his team complained about him. He thought he was being friendly by making comments about the clothes and bodies of the young women in his office. He would stomp around one day in a bad mood, shout at his staff and then the next day buy them all sweets and chocolates. This inconsistency meant that they all worked in dread that he'd arrive at work in a foul mood.

After professional coaching both of these people were able to resume managing people with an understanding of what is considered to be appropriate behaviour.

The effects of bullying

Bullying chips away a person's self-esteem. Many people blame themselves, thinking 'There must be something wrong with me.' This feeling of inadequacy can hook into any negative feelings that the victims may have about themselves stemming from childhood. People talk about 'rubber banding' back to a time when they were bullied as a child and now find that they have the same negative feelings.

People talk about feeling helpless and powerless when they have been bullied. As one woman stated in an interview with me: 'She totally shattered my confidence.'

One of Adams's (1992) clients described the effect of being bullied as: 'It makes you feel inadequate. It tells you things you're not very proud of, like accepting what's happening to you even though you know its wrong. But it's a trap. Because you have to earn a living, you don't tell.'

People can feel isolated. Rayner (1997) found bullying to be one of the major stressors in organisations and Cooper and Cartwright (1996), in his stress research, claims that one-third of work-related stress may be caused by bullying at work.

People feel demeaned and devalued and this can affect the way they see not only themselves but also their work and their families. Consequently, the tense relationships at home result in rows, anger and withdrawal followed by the victim's sense of isolation and feelings of guilt about upsetting the people they love.

In the short term people suffer the ill-health effects of stress from being bullied physiologically and psychologically. Later these effects can be demonstrated behaviourally. The physiological effects of stress include headaches, migraine, nausea, skin rashes, irritable bowel syndrome, increased blood pressure, sweating and a churning stomach. The short-term psychological symptoms include anxiety, panic attacks, tearfulness, a constant feeling of dread and depression.

The behavioural manifestations are often obvious. Someone previously outgoing may appear withdrawn and irritable. They no longer want to socialise with friends. They may become defensive or aggressive and blame those around them for the way that they are feeling.

One member of staff whose response to being bullied was to stay in bed and hide was soon being chased by Human Resources for his attendance record.

People under stress can change their habits and begin smoking, drinking or eating more then usual. Often, they stop taking care of themselves to the extent that their appearance changes; they may even stop bothering to exercise in the way that they did in the past.

The long-term effects of being bullied at work are that people can 'burn out' and have to take long-term sick leave. A senior college lecturer told Savva (1997):

> The certain knowledge that I was being judged negatively whatever I did or did not do, caused me considerable mental anguish. At home, I grew to be argumentative and short-tempered, unable to sleep and I fell into alcohol and prescription drug abuse. My confidence and competence as a teacher disintegrated.

Zapf and Gustafsson, quoted in Zapf and Leymann (1996), found that of the 64 people studied as a result of continual workplace bullying, 59 were suffering from post-traumatic stress disorder. The other five were suffering from a burn-out syndrome.

People can suffer serious long-term depression or anxiety disorders. One woman working in a caring profession realised that she was unable to cope any longer with the bullying from her senior manager. After one particularly vicious phone call she was rushed to coronary care.

People can be driven to commit suicide. This can take a number of forms, such as slowly stopping to take care of themselves, having an accident or turning to a deliberate aggressive act of taking their life.

Marriages break up and families fall apart, especially if the person doesn't identify what is happening to them and finds it easier to blame someone who is closer to them for the way that they are feeling.

A woman who came to see me was being bullied consistently by her line manager, who happened to be a drinking buddy of the directors. This left my client feeling impotent; she lost her voice totally for a period of two weeks and no physiological cause could be found.

Some bullying behaviours are so gross that it is not recommended that the victim speak to the perpetrator for fear of escalating the situation and making the person feel even worse about themselves.

Post-traumatic stress disorder

People can suffer from post-traumatic stress disorder (PTSD) as a result of having been bullied at work, reliving the worst incidents in flashbacks or nightmares and generally being in constant fear of the stressor. This may be the result of one particular incident or may be the build-up of years of subtler bullying and abuse. One woman drove miles out of town to do her shopping for fear of bumping into the woman who had been bullying her for several years.

Symptoms can be divided into three groups; first is the re-experiencing of the traumatic events in dreams or flashbacks or by acting out the event. These symptoms can just happen to the individual with no apparent trigger or they are triggered by something that is, on the surface, innocuous. The triggers can be olfactory: one client felt sick whenever she would smell the particular perfume worn by her female boss who had bullied her in subtle ways for years. Visual triggers are also common; seeing a car of the same model and colour as the one driven by the man who bullied her makes another client break out in a cold sweat. In another case, a man who no longer works in the same department as his boss who made his life hell for years will walk the long route around the building and even risk being late if he should hear 'that voice' talking to someone else. There is also the woman who wants to scream if someone puts their hand on her shoulder, which makes her return to being that terrified office junior who was the victim of the senior manager's unwanted attention.

The second group includes avoiding thoughts, feelings or activities associated with the events. This can really affect a person's everyday life because it means avoiding ordinary things such as public transport or public areas such as the canteen in case they encounter the bully. One woman who had been bullied by someone in the media felt that she could not escape, they were always on television and radio and in the popular magazines.

The third group of symptoms involves increased arousal, which causes problems of relaxing, going to sleep, outbursts of anger, hypervigilance and exaggerated startle response. Research by Davidson et al. (1990) found that PTSD patients suffered the associated problems of high levels of alcohol and other substance abuse, anxiety, depression and relationship difficulties.

See Appendix I for a more detailed account of the symptoms of PTSD.

Accidents

According to research carried out by the Health and Safety Executive, people who are being bullied are more likely to make mistakes and lose concentration because they are constantly anxious and thinking about the distressing events. They are more likely to have accidents, ranging from minor incidents such as stepping off a kerb and spraining an ankle, or burning themselves while cooking, to more serious car accidents.

The Health and Safety Executive research stated further that the costs to organisations are high in terms of increased absenteeism, low motivation, reduced productivity and efficiency.

The link between bullying and stress means that people make hasty decisions – and consequently mistakes – and the result is poor industrial relations.

Inability to fight back

You may be wondering why these people stay in these dreadful situations. There is a variety of reasons. Often, initially, people do not recognise what is happening to them and it takes an outsider, such as a friend or a professional, to actually say, 'You are being bullied.' Until this point, they had probably thought that there was something wrong with themselves. Other people stay because of loyalty to their company, their colleagues, or, in the case of health professionals, their patients.

Some victims of bullying are the family breadwinners in a geographical area where alternative employment is scarce, and besides this, once their self-esteem is low from being bullied they think 'who else would employ me?' They may be afraid to admit to their families that they have problems at work for fear of causing them stress, or they may even not want to admit it to themselves.

Chapter 5

Employers, harassment, bullying and the law

Introduction

This book is not just about identifying the dark or shadow side of organisational life; even more crucially it is also about providing ways to confront and solve the problems that arise with the minimum of stress, disruption and cost to all concerned.

Whereas previously the problems of harassment and bullying may have been thought of as matters for large corporations, the way in which members of staff are treated now needs to be taken seriously no matter what the size of the organisation.

I have heard comments like 'We don't worry about policies here. We are too small and, besides, nothing like that has ever occurred here.' This comment was made by the managing director of a small company whose idea of management was 'If you don't like it, you know where the door is.' The reality was that his employees were terrified of him. The company was located in a very small town in which there was a shortage of jobs. To his credit, he paid people above the minimum wage, but he expected to be treated like a god in return.

Fortunately, the law increasingly frowns upon this and we have seen over the last few years an upsurge in successful litigation.

It is clear that employees who suffer from bullying or harassment in the workplace now have a number of potential legal remedies open to them, and that employers are increasingly likely to be found liable following such claims. There is scope not only for significant financial awards, but also for criminal liability on the part of perpetrators, management and company directors.

From the employer's point of view, litigation can mean increased financial and legal costs, damage to their public reputation, greater difficulty in recruitment efforts, and adverse effects on profits.

It is true to say that most potential legal cases do not receive publicity as they are settled out of court. Because only the most extreme cases reach the courts, what we read about in the news-papers is probably only the tip of the iceberg. However, even when cases reach a negotiated settlement, the costs are considerable in terms of time, money, stress and damage to staff morale.

As far as the victims are concerned, many do not feel they can be compensated for their suffering by mere financial compensation. One man arrived at my consulting room clutching a cheque for more money than any court would have awarded him and yet this made no difference to his shattered self-esteem. He had gone into a privately owned company as the assistant to the MD but had quickly come to understand that he had no power and was merely the next target for the MD's bullying behaviours. This man was verbally abused, humiliated in front of customers and undermined in front of other staff. He was then told that in dealing with discipline matters he was inadequate. Why did he stay? The reasons are many. He had moved his wife and family to this country, and though he had given up a good and secure job in his country of origin he thought it was he who had problems. If he could just change his ways and be what his boss wanted him to be, he thought he might just make it work. It was only when he was pushed into a state of physical and psychological collapse that he gave in. A cheque was written and given to him the same day along with his P45 and exit papers.

Statutory remedies against employers

Because harassment is perpetrated on grounds such as gender, race and disability, some legislation is directly relevant to dealing with harassment at work. These are the Sex Discrimination Act, the Race Relations Act and the Disability Discrimination Act.

The Sex Discrimination Acts of 1975 and 1976

The 1975 Act described sexual harassment as a 'particularly degrading and unacceptable form of treatment which it must be taken to have been the intention to restrain.'

This Act makes it unlawful to discriminate against any person, either directly or indirectly, in the area of employment on the grounds of sex or marital status. This means that it is unlawful to discriminate on this basis in:

- deciding who is offered a job (this includes discrimination in advertising the position and granting interviews to candidates),
- the terms and conditions on which the job is offered,
- providing opportunities for promotion, transfer and training,
- providing benefits, facilities or services granted to employees, and
- dismissal or other unfavourable treatment of employees.

A guide issued by the Trade Union Congress (TUC) in 1983, defined sexual harassment as:

- unnecessary touching or physical contact,
- suggestive remarks or other verbal abuse,
- leering at a person's body,
- compromising invitations,
- demands for sexual favours, and
- physical assault.

Other definitions include the circulation or display of offensive material, jokes or comments about dress or appearance, and provocation. In its most extreme form it would include rape.

The Employment Appeal Tribunal (EAT) directed industrial tribunals to have regard to Recommendation 191-131 EEC on the protection of dignity of men and women at work when hearing cases involving allegations of sexual harassment. The Recommendation seeks to define the term 'sexual harassment' as:

Unwanted conduct of a sexual nature, or other conduct based on sex affecting the dignity of women and men at work. This can include unwelcome physical, verbal or non-verbal conduct.

The Race Relations Act of 1976

Discrimination on racial grounds includes discrimination on the basis of colour, nationality, citizenship, race, and ethnic or national origins. The Act applies to Great Britain, but not Northern Ireland. In employment it is unlawful to discriminate on this basis:

- in deciding who is offered a job (this includes discrimination in advertising the position and instructions to recruiters or agencies),
- in relation to any terms of employment offered,
- by refusing or deliberately omitting to offer a person employment,
- in providing opportunities for promotion, transfer or training,
- in providing of benefits, facilities or services,
- in dismissals or other unfavourable treatment, and
- segregation, i.e., separating one person or group of people from another.

Harassment on the grounds of race and sex constitutes unfavourable and discriminatory treatment. The individual or individuals concerned may be said to have suffered a 'detriment'.

The Disability Discrimination Act of 1995

This Act prohibits discrimination by an employer against a disabled person at every stage of employment (i.e., in recruitment, promotion, training, working conditions and dismissal). A disabled person is described by the Act as someone with a physical or mental impairment that has a long-term and substantial effect on their ability to carry out normal, day-to-day activities.

The employment provisions of the Act apply to United Kingdom employers with more than 15 employees. In 1997 the Government commenced a review of the small-business exemptions with a view to reducing the threshold from 20 (as it then was) to 15, 10, 5 or 2 employees, removing it altogether by 2004.

The Act states at paragraph 6.22 that: 'Harassing a disabled person on account of disability will almost always amount to a "detriment" under the Act.'

Employers' liability under criminal law

Under criminal law, there are now a number of remedies, applicable to harassment and bullying, which are available.

The Protection from Harassment Act of 1997

This Act is primarily designed to address one particular type of harassment – stalking. However, it affects other types of harassment, including that in the workplace.

Two criminal offences are recognised: the offence of harassment and the offence of putting people in fear of violence. Section 1(1) provides that:

> A person must not pursue a course of conduct–
> (a) which amounts to harassment of another, and
> (b) which he knows or ought to know amounts to harassment of the other.

Section 1(2) states further:

> A person whose course of conduct is in question ought to know that it amounts to harassment of another if a reasonable person in possession of the same information would think the course of conduct amounted to harassment of the other.

Section 7 of the Act provides that:

> – references to harassing a person include alarming the person or causing the person distress;
> – a 'course of conduct' must involve conduct on at least two occasions;
> – 'conduct' includes speech.

The offence of putting people in fear of violence is provided for in Section 4(1) and (2) as follows:

> A person whose course of conduct causes another to fear, on at least two occasions, that violence will be used against him is guilty of an offence if he knows or ought to know that his course of conduct will cause the other so to fear on each of those occasions.
>
> The person whose course of conduct is in question ought to know that it will cause another to fear that violence will be used against him on any occasion if a reasonable person in

possession of the same information would think that the course of conduct would cause the other so to fear on that occasion.

The Criminal Justice and Public Order Act of 1994

This Act inserted a new clause (4A) into the Public Order Act of 1986 and created a new criminal offence of intentional harassment, which could potentially be used in cases of harassment or bullying. Section 4A(1) provides:

> A person is guilty of an offence if, with intent to cause a person harassment, alarm or distress, he/she
>   (a) uses threatening, abusive or insulting words or behaviour, or disorderly behaviour; or
>   (b) displays any writing, sign or other visible representation which is threatening abusive or insulting, thereby causing that or another person harassment, alarm or distress.

Seward (1998) notes that the definition requires proof that the perpetrator 'intended' to cause harassment. Section 4A(2) makes it clear that the offence can be committed in public or private places but excludes private dwellings. Therefore, the workplace is not excluded. The legislation is primarily intended to help the police deal more effectively with serious cases of racial harassment, however, as the wording of the section is wide; the word 'harassment' in this context does not require the behaviour to be on the grounds of race, sex or disability.

Seward (1998) further points out that as a result of this legislation employers need to be clear both in their policy documents and when giving training in the field of harassment and bullying awareness that employees found guilty of harassment of their colleagues may face serious criminal sanctions.

The Health and Safety at Work Act of 1978

Some bullying cases may come under the Health and Safety at Work Act, which states that all employers have a duty to take whatever steps are necessary to ensure the health, safety and welfare of their employees.

Section 2(i) prescribes that to comply with this duty an employer must provide:

- a safe place to work;
- safe means of access to that place of work;
- a safe system of work;
- adequate materials;
- competent colleagues;
- protection from unnecessary risk or injury.

This Act defines personal injury as 'any disease or impairment of a person's physical or mental health in the workplace'.

Because the Act holds it to be the responsibility of the employer to ensure the health, safety and welfare of all its work employees, liability for bullying could be contemplated under all three of these categories. For example, the statute requires a safe system of work to be provided. This implies that unreasonable pressure, deadlines and demands are unlikely to be considered safe; thus, where risks to health (such as stress and stress-related illness) occur, an employer could be in breach of this Act.

Furthermore, the legislation places an obligation on the employer to protect employees against unnecessary risk of injury. Bullying clearly exposes individuals to risks of injury, whether psychological or where the employee has a known medical condition.

According to Section 7, every employee, while at work, is to:

- take reasonable care for his own health and safety;
- take reasonable care for the health and safety of others who may be affected by what he does or does not do at work;
- co-operate with his employer, or with any other person, on whom a duty is imposed, so far as it is necessary for it to be complied with.

Ashton (1999) states that this is wide enough to cover the employee's responsibility to take care of his own psychological well-being while at work, as well as the duty to take care of others. Although there have been numerous prosecutions in respect of physical risks and harm, he suggests that the future is open to prosecution for psychological risks and harm.

Section 33 provides that it is a criminal offence not to comply with the Act. Section 37 provides that senior members of a company such as directors and managers may be prosecuted if the breach of the Act is committed with their 'consent or connivance' or was attributable to any neglect on their part. Therefore where an employer does not take adequate steps to eradicate bullying and harassment in the workplace, then certainly in serious cases there may be potential liability under this Act for both employer and senior management.

It needs to be borne in mind, however, that the criminal law is more concerned with tackling the offence or offender, rather than helping the victim. The onus is on the victim employee to report the bully to the Police or the British Health and Safety Executive (HSE) and is then reliant upon the Crown Prosecution Service or HSE to take action. One of the problems is that the standard of proof is higher in a criminal case than in a civil action (i.e., beyond reasonable doubt). Another problem is that there is no assurance that the case will be pursued because the police may contend that it is more appropriately a civil case. Finally, even if a criminal action does proceed, it is unlikely to bring about reconciliation between the parties involved.

Remedies against the employer under common law

Other possible routes against the employer could be common-law remedies referred to as tortious claims (i.e., civil wrongs). The common law imposes upon employers a duty of care in the tort of negligence for the health and safety of its employees. This means that they have a duty of care to provide a safe system of work and competent employees with whom to work. In consequence both harassment and bullying could be viewed as a potential workplace hazard. Tortious damages can include sums in respect of injury to feelings, medical expenses, certain intangible losses and emotional distress.

Seward (1998) predicts that the law of negligence is likely to become a major influence on the practices of employers in relation to stress. The risk of legal exposure will also increase the need to incorporate expressly into contracts the concept of dignity at work to enable organisations to control the acts of their employees.

A further possible recourse for an employee who suffers harassment or bullying at work could be a claim for breach of contract.

Seward (1998) suggests that 'Such a claim could be brought on the basis of the implied terms; that an employer will provide a safe system of work; that an employee will not be harassed or bullied by the employer or by fellow employees in the course of their employment and of the implied duty of mutual trust and confidence.'

One case, which illustrated such a claim, is *Waltons & Morse* v. *Dorrington* (1997) IRLR 488. The Employment Appeal Tribunal (EAT) stated that it is an implied term of every contract of employment:

> That the employer will provide and monitor for his employees, so far as is reasonably practicable, a working environment which is reasonably suitable for the performance by them of their contractual duties.

The facts of this case concerned a smoke-free working environment. However, the concept of a suitable working environment as stated in this case is sufficiently wide to include a duty by the employer to protect an employee from harassment and bullying in the workplace.

Seward (1998) views the case has having particular significance in relation to serial bullying, where a failure to treat seriously, and investigate fully, any complaint of bullying or harassment and/or failure to give reasonable support to a victim 'is likely to constitute a repudiatory breach of that term whether or not any independent duty of dignity can be said to exist in the contract'.

The case of *Walker* v. *Northumberland County Council* (1995) emphasised a 'duty of care'. The Council was found to have 'acted unreasonably and in breach of its duty to care' in continuing to employ Mr Walker after he had suffered a nervous breakdown and failing to provide him with assistance. It was stated that the Council should have known or that it was reasonable for them to have known that returning him to the same job with no extra support might mean that he could suffer a second breakdown. Indeed, the additional stress did cause a second breakdown.

This ground-breaking decision recognised that employers do have a duty of care for employees' psychological health and opened the doors to litigation against employers by employees who suffer extreme stress after being harassed or bullied in the workplace. Consequently, bullying behaviour would constitute a breach of the employer's duty of care under the Health and Safety at Work Act.

If, after an issue of this sort has been brought to the attention of the employer, it chooses not to take action, the employer will be in breach of this Act.

However, early in 2002 the Court of Appeal set out tough new guidelines for people claiming damages for job-related stress. The Court ruled that signs of stress in a worker must be plain enough that any reasonable employer should realise that something needs to be done about it. Lord Justice Hale said: 'If there is no alternative solution, it has to be for the employee to decide whether or not to carry on in the same employment and take the risk of a breakdown in his health or whether to leave that employment and look for work elsewhere before he becomes unemployable.'

The judges in these cases indicated that any employer who offers a confidential counselling advice service with access to treatment is unlikely to be found in breach of duty.

In response to these judgements, the TUC senior health and safety officer, Owen Tudor, said: 'We will make sure our members know that the Court of Appeal has urged them not to suffer in silence but get their complaints about bullying, overwork, inadequate training and unrealistic deadlines on record.'

A spokesman for Unison said: 'Employers do have a duty of care and a legal obligation to carry out risk assessments, to consider how working conditions affect not only the physical but also the psychological health of their employees.'

The British Health and Safety Executive (HSE) has published guidance for employers on the prevention of stress at work, which states that bullying can be a cause of stress and that preventative measures must include action to eliminate bullying where it exists.

In June 2001 the HSE published new best-practice guidelines on how to minimise stress in the workplace. Under the guidelines, employers must:

- identify the hazards,
- decide who could be harmed and how,
- evaluate the risk,
- record significant findings, and
- review the assessment at regular intervals.

Clearly, identifying and dealing with bullying at work comes under the jurisdiction of these best-practice guidelines.

Employers can also be liable for the actions of their employees against each other. The Andrea Adams Trust (2000) states:

> Where authorised behaviour (such as giving instructions and orders to subordinates), was done in an unauthorised way (for example, in a demeaning, humiliating or insulting or oppressive manner) the employer may well be held liable.

What this suggests is that employers may not be able to avoid liability on the grounds that they delegated their duty to someone else. For example, in *McDermott* v. *Nash Dredging and Reclamation Co Ltd.* (1987) IC R 9127, the court stated:

> An employer owed to his employees a duty to exercise reasonable care to ensure that the system of work provided for him was a safe one. The essential characteristic is that it is no defence for the employer to show that he delegated its performance to a person, whether his servant or not his servant, whom he reasonably believed to be competent to perform it. Despite such delegation, the employer is liable for the non-performance of the duty.

Consequently, if the employer knew – or should reasonably have known – of stress or bullying, this would constitute an unsafe practice and would be open to liability.

The Public Interest Disclosure Act (1998) is often called the 'Whistleblowing Act'. In effect, this Act compels employers to ensure that any allegations or complaints made by workers are taken seriously. Employee rights under the Act are enforceable in an Employment Tribunal, and the Department of Employment has announced that there will be no statutory limit on compensation awarded.

When assessing the validity of the worker's disclosure, one factor that will certainly be taken into account is whether the worker has complied with any procedure authorised by the employer for making such a disclosure.

From the point of view of the employer, this makes it essential to establish a clearly defined policy for both internal and external disclosure for employees. Any policy should include a clear statement that malpractice is taken very seriously in the organisation and should clearly define what these malpractices are and how they should be dealt with.

The future

On a wider scale, in 1996 the MSF Union put together the Dignity at Work Bill, which Lord Monkswell steered through the House of Lords. It had been blocked by John Major's Conservative government in February 1997, when attempts were made to introduce it to House of Commons shortly before the General Election was announced. The Bill has been on hold ever since.

The Bill proposes an Act to provide for a right of dignity at work for employees and for connected purposes. Section 1 of the Bill states:

1   Every employee shall have a right to dignity at work and if the terms of the contract under which a person is employed do not include that right they shall be deemed to include it.

2   Subject to section 5 of this Act, an employer commits a breach of the right to dignity at work of an employee if that employee suffers during his employment with the employer harassment or bullying or any act, omission or conduct which causes him to be alarmed or distressed including but not limited to any of the following –

   (a) behaviour on more than one occasion which is offensive, abusive, malicious, insulting or intimidating;

   (b) unjustified criticism on more than one occasion;

   (c) punishment imposed without reasonable justification, or

   (d) changes in the duties or responsibilities of the employee to the employee's detriment without reasonable justification.

One of the major effects of such legislation being passed is that all employees – including those at smaller companies – will be afforded protection against the tyranny of the bully at work. In Chapter 6 the proposals of the Dignity at Work Bill regarding the contents of a dignity at work policy are discussed.

A positive example for our own legislators to follow is that of the State of Queensland, Australia, where Premier Peter Beattie is intent on cracking down on bullying at work (see Chapter 2).

Dignity at Work policies

Introduction

The success of an organisational policy on harassment is dependent on its being both accessible and understandable by all employees. When I have asked employees what their company policy says, all too often they tell me that they don't know whether one exists – and even if it did, they would have no idea where to find it.

Some organisations may already have a good policy in place, but if the awareness of it is low it simply needs to be relaunched. Other organisations will need to write their policy from scratch.

Any organisation whose employees have the support of a union needs to involve the union in any policy writing and updating. The union can provide invaluable support for both the organisation and the workers. The consensus of all parties involved facilitates both launching and implementing a policy.

Any organisation that does not have an official policy on bullying in the workplace needs to launch one. All senior personnel and anyone with management responsibility require specific training in how the policy works and how its importance should be cascaded down to their staff. Naturally, every new member of staff joining the organisation should receive a copy of the policy and if the new person is taking a management role they need training as well. On an annual basis, all personnel should be given a copy of the updated policy. Many organisations post their corporate policies on their company-wide intranet for easy access.

Many larger organisations have members of staff trained as 'harassment advisers'. These people take on an extra responsibility to talk to members of the organisation who feel that they are being bullied and harassed in some way. They can help them to understand the policy and identify their options, and explain to them the different procedures they can follow. These people serve a useful role within an organisation as they can often help colleagues to identify and label why they are feeling unhappy in their jobs, unwell or even particularly stressed. They also take the initial load off the HR department who can intervene at a later stage should that be necessary. The harassment adviser role is usually confidential unless the individual employee wants to take it further.

A well-written Dignity at Work policy has value only if the entire workforce is genuinely committed to implementing it – from the senior management team downwards. This is demonstrated by the case of *Canniffe* v. *East Riding of Yorkshire Council* EOR 93 EAT (reported in *Employer's Law*, November 2000) which suggests that the mere existence of a well-written policy is not necessarily sufficient. The facts were as follows:

> Canniffe bought a sex discrimination claim after suffering from serious incidents of harassment and sexual assault by K. The Council accepted it was vicariously liable for K's conduct, but relied on the statutory defence that it had taken steps as were reasonably practicable to prevent it occurring by putting in place a harassment policy that was drawn to all employees' attention. The tribunal found that no improvement in the implementation of the policy would have prevented K's conduct, and the claim was dismissed.
>
> Canniffe appealed successfully. The EAT held that in establishing whether the statutory defence was available the tribunal should have first identified whether the council had taken any steps at all to prevent K's behaviour, and should have gone on to consider whether the Council could have taken steps that were reasonably practicable, irrespective of whether or not those steps would have prevented the harassment. A harassment policy in itself was not enough.

This case highlights the danger of the complacency with which some organisations consider themselves protected from litigation by assuming 'We are OK, we have a policy.'

In truth, organisations sometimes have to take serious, conscious and often unpalatable steps to eradicate this behaviour – such as sometimes having to dismiss senior or key personnel who fail to treat other people properly. Organisations therefore need to acknowledge that *they* are responsible for the way in which members of their staff treat one other.

The content of a Dignity at Work policy

The Dignity at Work Bill (see Chapter 5) lays out clearly what should be included in a Dignity at Work policy. Relevant extracts are reproduced below:

Schedule 1

Dignity at Work policy

1   In order to comply with section 5 of this Act an employer's Dignity at Work policy must comply with the provisions of this Schedule.

2   The Dignity at Work Policy must be in writing and distributed to every employee and must include the following:

   (a) an explanation of the statutory right of all employees to dignity at work and a statement that breaches of that right will not be tolerated;

   (b) examples of the types of behaviour which do not conform with the right to dignity at work and of conduct which may lead to disciplinary action;

   (c) a clear statement of the procedure for bringing complaints and the manner in which they will be dealt with which must include a commitment that complaints of a breach of the right to dignity at work will be taken seriously, investigated objectively and dealt with in confidence and must allow the complainant to be represented by a representative of his choice at all stages;

   (d) designation of a competent person to whom complaints should be made and who shall fulfil the functions allotted to the competent person within the meaning of this Act;

   (e) a clear statement of the disciplinary procedure to be followed against employees who infringe the Policy, which shall comply with the provision of the ACAS Code of Practice on Disciplinary Practice and Procedure in Employment (1997);

(f) details (including names and contact telephone numbers) of designated persons available to counsel, assist and advise individuals bringing complaints or those who are the subject of complaints;

(g) arrangements to train in the Policy all those occupying any position of managerial authority with the employer and to inform all employees of the Policy;

(h) annual monitoring of the operation of the Policy, to be reported to senior management and to include a summary of all complaints made under the Policy (with names of complainants kept confidential unless the complainant agrees); and

(i) arrangements for consultation with trade union and safety representatives on the operation of the Policy, its implementation and any revision of the Policy in the light of its operation in practice.

Launching a policy

Once a policy has been formulated with the senior management team and, where appropriate, agreed with the union body, it is time for the policy to be launched. An important element of this process is the presentation of the policy to everyone within the organisation.

The following section can be used as a checklist covering the various stages in launching the policy.

All such presentations should include:

- What is dignity at work?
- What is bullying?
- Why do we need a policy?
- The impact of harassment on the individual and the organisation.
- Harassment, bullying and the law.

Consider sending out a questionnaire to all personnel asking questions such as:

- What is your understanding of dignity at work?
- When you hear the term 'harassment and bullying' what do you think of?

- Do you believe that harassment and bullying goes on in the organisation?
- Have you personally been harassed or bullied within this organisation?

The following steps should be undertaken:

1 Present the policy in its entirety to the senior management team.
2 Train the senior management team in the workings of the policy and ensure they understand their roles.
3 Train all personnel and human resources staff in how the policy works and what their roles will be.
4 Train managers and deputy managers and inform them of their role. Find out about any discomfort or reservations they might have about implementing the policy.
5 Inform all staff to whom the policy applies both via leaflet and the intranet (if appropriate). Pin flyers and posters to staff notice boards and include reminders with pay-slips.
6 Make sure all new staff receive policy information with their joining pack.
7 Arrange compulsory training seminars for all personnel.
8 Ensure all staff are aware that the policy is not just another piece of paper but that the organisation takes dignity at work seriously.
9 Collect statistics of bullying at work (e.g., instances, resolutions, etc.) and agree to publish the findings.

Any informal complaint should be turned around within a week and formal complaints should aim to be completed within two weeks (subject to witness availability).

There are excellent video and written materials available to help train personnel (see Appendix II).

Sample Dignity at Work policy

The following is an example of a Dignity at Work policy. Every organisation has its own unique characteristics and needs; therefore policy-makers will make amendments accordingly. For example, in some organisations the first stage may be to seek advice from a harassment counsellor; in others HR or a line manager may be the only option.

This sample policy is intended, ideally, to form part of a much larger document including the Equal Opportunities policy, disciplinary matters, etc. It is designed, however, to stand alone, if that is what the circumstances warrant.

DIGNITY AT WORK

S Y N O P S I S

1 Introduction

All employees have a right to be treated with dignity and respect at their place of work. They have a right to work in an environment free from harassment and bullying by anyone. Any breach of an individual's rights will be dealt with under the company's discipline procedure and could result in dismissal.

Bullying is offensive, intimidating, malicious, insulting or humiliating behaviour, abuse of power or authority which attempts to undermine an individual or group of employees and which may cause them to suffer stress.

Harassment is unwelcome conduct of a physical, verbal or non-verbal nature which the recipient finds offensive, intimidating or hostile and which affects their dignity at work.

Harassment and bullying is not about what the perpetrator meant; it is what the recipient felt – i.e., impact and not intention is the criterion.

Harassment, bullying and victimisation *will not* be tolerated under any circumstances within this organisation and will be treated as a disciplinary offence.

Harassment, bullying and victimisation include comments, actions and jokes that contribute to a stressful working environment, whether physical, verbal or non-verbal (e.g., printed materials such as posters, e-mails and text messages, gestures, the giving of unsolicited or unwanted gifts, voice mail, taped messages and anything said about a person and within their hearing). Harassment and bullying behaviours include either persistent or single incidents towards one or more employees.

Behaviours of corporate bullying under the guise of a 'tough management style' will not be tolerated.

2 Policy

This policy is applicable to anyone employed by this company and engaged in company business. This company offers all of its employees equality of opportunity. Every person employed by this organisation, no matter what their status, has a right to be treated with dignity and respect. They have a right to work in an environment free from unwelcome and inappropriate behaviour.

[Link the policy to the company's health and safety-at-work policy.]

- Every individual member of staff has a duty to ensure that this policy is adhered to and to treat other people – whether fellow employees or clients – with respect.
- The policy prohibits any form of harassment, bullying or victimisation.
- The policy covers all circumstances in which inappropriate behaviours could occur whether during working hours and on company premises or private property, or outside working hours in circumstances connected to the company, such as social events or conferences, on or off site.
- This company will take complaints or breaches of this policy seriously and will investigate expediently.
- Action consistent with the Discipline and Grievance Procedures will be taken against any employee, irrespective of status, who has been found to have breached this policy.
- Victimisation of any employee making a complaint of harassment or bullying will be taken seriously and the perpetrators

dealt with under the Discipline and Grievance Procedures.

- This company actively encourages individuals to deal with incidents with unwanted behaviour.
- This company ensures that all complaints will be handled confidentially, fairly and swiftly.
- The management team takes responsibility for reviewing and monitoring this policy.
- Confidential counselling will be provided for those being bullied or harassed and those accused of harassment.

3 Procedures for resolution of complaints

The aim of this procedure is to stop inappropriate behaviour occurring within the organisation. Anyone who receives a complaint of inappropriate behaviour that is occurring or has occurred in the organisation should not ignore it but take it seriously.

3.1 Support

It is acknowledged that due to the sensitive nature of some complaints and the status of some of the perpetrators the normal channel of talking directly to an individual's line manager may not be appropriate.

This company has trained the following people as advisers.

| [Tim Bloggs] | [Accounts dept] | ext 5342 |
| [Jane Public] | [IT admin] | ext 5677 |

These people will listen to you in confidence (off site if necessary) and help you to understand the company policy and make a decision about which route you wish to take. You will be advised to keep a diary of incidences of behaviour and attempts you have made to stop this behaviour.

3.2 Informal procedure

This company wants effective, confidential and speedy resolutions. Using the informal procedure guidelines any individual who feels that they have been harassed, bullied, victimised or treated in an inappropriate way may take the following informal actions:

1   *Ask the perpetrator to stop the behaviour.* It is recommended that the person does not do this alone and engages a third person to act as both a witness and support. Politely and respectfully point out the behaviours that are causing offence, the impact they are having on you and the effect on your work productivity. The perpetrator should be informed as soon as possible after the incident.

2   *Put the complaint in writing to the perpetrator(s)* stating clearly the nature of the behaviour, when and where it happened and the effect it had on you. State clearly that you want this behaviour to stop. Keep a dated copy.

3   *Ask a colleague to speak to the perpetrators on your behalf.* Ask them to explain the nature of the unwanted behaviour, its effect on you and that it has to stop.

4   *Discuss the situation with a member of the HR team, your supervisor or line manager* and ask them to speak to the perpetrator. Frequently, the above steps are sufficient to stop the inappropriate behaviour, especially if the perpetrator was genuinely unaware of the effect of their behaviour on others.

Wherever possible keep notes of the specific events, dates, times, circumstances, etc. Take these to a line manager or HR. They will explain your options under the policy.

3.3 Formal procedures
Informal procedures are not a substitute for formal procedures if

- you prefer the formal option, or
- the complaint is of a serious nature.

You may feel that a formal procedure is your only recourse if previous attempts at informal resolutions have proved unsuccessful.

Issues of harassment, bullying and victimisation can be raised at any time either orally or in writing. Managers, supervisors, team leaders and HR representatives have a responsibility to act quickly and take the matter forward once they have been made aware of behaviours that breach the policy.

You will be notified at this initial stage that you will have to recount the incidents in detail. You are entitled to be accompanied by a workplace friend/colleague or a trade union representative.

In normal circumstances, you, the complainant, make the decision to progress the complaint. In some circumstances, where the behaviour contravenes the company's health and safety policy, the company will make the decision to take action.

Note that in cases where an individual is so traumatised by an event that they feel they cannot take part in the investigation, a senior member of staff may stand in for them.

3.3.1 Instigating the formal procedure

All complaints must be made in writing and given to the line manager, departmental manager or HR representative. This report should be accompanied by any other evidence (e.g. letters, cards, printed copies of e-mail, tape-recordings of voice mail, etc.). In addition, details of any action taken to date, for example:

26 July 2002 – discussed distress with supervisor
29 July 2002 – asked person to stop

All written complaints will be handled expediently by a senior manager, who will appoint an investigator either internally or externally. The person appointed will have no previous involvement with the case.

The person(s) accused of the offence will be informed immediately that a written complaint has been received and an investigation is taking place under formal procedures. They must also be told that they will be informed in writing of the date and time of the formal meeting. Where possible, this should take place within five working days.

Both parties will be asked to keep the whole issue confidential within the organisation (apart from their own supporter and union representative).

In some cases where the parties work closely together it may be necessary to separate them until the investigation is completed. Usually, the victim is allowed to remain at home.

As a consequence of the outcome of the investigation the company may invoke its grievance and disciplinary procedure.

Many company policy documents contain an Appendix addressed to employees who think they may be (or are being) bullied at work. This guidance could also be circulated to the workforce in other ways, but in any event should adhere to the following basic guidelines.

APPENDIX
What to do if you are being bullied at work

1   Don't ignore it. It is unlikely to stop and as much as you want or pray for the bully to leave, they are unlikely to do so.
2   Find out if your company has a written policy that covers harassment and bullying. If it has the procedures to follow, these should be clearly laid out.
3   Log all incidents of bullying: dates, time, nature of the incident, etc. Write down actual words used and stick to the facts.
4   Note your feelings and what you said or did, if anything.
5   Write down the names of any witnesses who were present or within earshot at the time, even if you don't think they would speak up for you.
6   Keep copies of any written materials, letters, e-mails, faxes, etc. that are offensive and would constitute bullying.
7   Ask a colleague to accompany you to ask the bully to stop behaving in this way towards you.
8   If you feel you cannot confront the bully, send them a memo stating the nature of the behaviour and the effects it is having on you and ask them to stop. Keep a copy of this document safely, preferably at home but in any case away from your work site.
9   Report the incidents to a supervisor or line manager. If it is the supervisor or line manager who is the one bullying you, go directly to Human Resources.
10 If applicable, ask your union representative for guidance.

Chapter 7

Harassment investigation

Under most policies, any formal complaint is required to be made in writing within three months of the alleged incidents. There are exceptions to this, for example where unacceptable behaviour is ongoing, or where the allegations concern serious and repeated acts of bullying against one individual or several people. In any event, once the complaint has been made, the next step is to investigate it.

Internal investigations

In Chapter 6 I touched briefly on the role of so-called harassment advisers and investigators. These are people who, in addition to their normal functions and activities in the company, have agreed to act as advisers to other staff members who feel they have been victimised. Harassment advisers and investigators are therefore not usually involved with other aspects of Human Resources administration and are generally scattered throughout the organisation.

Harassment advisers require specific training to work within the organisation's particular policy and tend to be effective in larger organisations where they can be drafted in from other sites, especially for investigation work. They also need to be trained in basic counselling skills such as:

- contracting for time and place,
- confidentiality contract,
- listening skills,
- questioning techniques,
- facilitating client decisions.

The harassment adviser will be asked questions such as:

- Do you think I'm making a fuss over nothing?
- What will happen to the bully if they are believed?
- How long will it all take?
- Will they believe me as they are more senior than me?
- Do you believe me?

Trained harassment advisers will listen to people who have been harassed or bullied at work, introduce them to the company's policies and explain how they work. Part of their role is to help them to identify whether the complaint falls within the ambit of the policy and, if it does, guide complainants through their options for dealing with it. Harassment advisers also act as a good referral source, either to line managers, HR, or an outside agency, such as the company's Employment Assistance Programme (EAP) provider. It is not their remit to take on a counsellor's role.

Advisers must remain impartial in order to be of most benefit to the complainant. For this reason they cannot work with both parties and must refer the second party to a colleague who has also been trained as an adviser.

Whichever party they see, the adviser should listen, refer back to the organisation's policy and advise on the next steps under the policy.

If the complainant decides to take an informal route, the adviser needs to point them in the direction of the appropriate manager to see. If, however, the complainant decides to take a formal course of action, the adviser needs to advise them on what is likely to happen and what will be expected of them.

I have found that the drawback to this arrangement is that after an organisation has carried out an internal investigation, it might receive a complaint from one of the parties concerned that the process was biased or unfair in some way. The whole exercise will then have to be repeated by an unbiased external investigator. In these cases the external investigator will need to see all the documentation from the initial investigation.

Outside consultants

For smaller organisations the use of outside investigators is invaluable. It avoids role conflict and other longer-term repercussions, such as holding grudges (either on someone's own, or another person's, behalf) and acting on them later.

The advantages of employing outside consultants are:

- they are objective and impartial;
- they have a good knowledge of organisations and the conflicts that can arise within them;
- they are experienced in the skills needed to conduct the investigation efficiently and with as little stress as possible, especially in sensitive situations;
- they have a sound understanding of the legal aspects;
- they have the know-how to access complex direct and indirect evidence;
- they are alert to any possibility of constructive resolution such as mediation;
- they have the sensitivity to know when an individual would benefit from being referred for individual counselling;
- they are trained in harassment investigation and are comfortable with the procedures;
- an experienced consultant will accompany any new investigator;
- in large-scale investigations, the external consultant can be used to lead a team of investigators;
- they do not have any preconceived ideas and have not been exposed to histories or rumours surrounding the people concerned;
- they do not have a history with the organisation and can assure confidentially.

The last point in the above list highlights a major disadvantage of using internal personnel for a mediation or harassment investigation in particular. Especially in smaller organisations with one office base, there is a whole mycelium of interpersonal relationships with people knowing, knowing of, or knowing someone related to others in the departments.

Sometimes I have been called into an organisation after internal attempts at resolving issues have failed. In one case the internal investigating officer was the ex-wife of the accused's brother. In another, the organisation was the only substantial employer in a small town and specifics of the issue were being gossiped about in the local supermarket. Confidentiality is essential in all organisational consultancy work.

Senior people often call in an outside consultant because they need to feel that there is someone who will be there for them and listen to them; they need someone to understand their dilemma and have sufficient objectivity to be able to help. The usual scenario is that the more senior the victim, the more sparse is their support system, and the more emotional support and practical help they will need.

When not actually locked into the organisational system it is easier for the consultant to see the bigger picture and comprehend the overall pattern emerging.

The illustrations in this book are taken from an idea given to me by a colleague, Sue. She calls them 'the litmus test'. The alleged bully needs to answer questions such as:

- Would you want your behaviour to be public knowledge?
- Would you want someone to treat your mother or wife in the way in which you have treated this woman?
- Would you like your new boyfriend to see the way in which you treat your junior members of staff?

I have lost count of the number of times an individual has sat in my consulting room and told me that they are useless, that they keep getting it wrong and that they cannot understand why. As the story unfolds with their telling me about the way in which they are being treated at work, I am invariably the one to put the label of 'bullying' on the behaviours of others towards them. The responses are usually a mixture of shock, relief and, frequently, tears. Most of us 'normal neurotics' find it easier to think that there is something wrong with ourselves before we think that there is something wrong with someone else.

I believe that the most important role that the professional can take in the early days is *to listen to the victim*. They need a space and opportunity to talk. Perhaps they have tried to discuss their problems at home, only to be told that they're always 'moaning about work'. Or, if not, maybe it is because they feel that no one would want to listen anyway. Allowing them to unburden themselves cannot be overestimated.

The process of the investigation

Briefing the investigator

The success of an investigation is totally dependent upon the brief given to the investigator by the HR department. In this section I am therefore addressing HR personnel directly.

First, the investigator will need a private room away from the main open-plan office, with an internal telephone, water and tissues.

Then, the investigator should be given copies of the complaint and any other evidence (copies of e-mails, voice mails, memos, letters, etc.), as well as any other relevant materials. If possible, the investigator should be familiar with your Equal Opportunities or Dignity at Work policies before your initial meeting with them. At the meeting, you should cover the following questions:

- Whom they should interview.
- Whether you want to give them the contact details and allow them to make their own appointments or do that for them.
- Where the interviews are to be carried out.
- The timescale.
- How the report should be presented (e.g., in written form only, in the form of a written report and a presentation in person to a panel or an individual within the organisation, etc.).
- The number of witnesses to be interviewed.
- Whether you require recommendations from the investigator.

It is usual for an organisation to allow the investigator to interview any people that either party chooses to call.

Stating your requirements clearly at the beginning and making a contract of agreement can avoid disappointment on either side later in the process.

Some investigators are happy to work alone and do their own note taking. Others may prefer to work in pairs, with one person acting as scribe. Sometimes investigators expect the organisation to provide a confidential scribe.

The investigation

1   The investigator will study all the paperwork; especially the written complaints and the written evidence. They will also listen to taped evidence.

2   The investigator will usually interview the person or persons making the complaints first. However, this is not essential if people are on holiday, etc.

3   The person or persons accused of the inappropriate behaviour will be interviewed as to the complaints brought against them.

4   The investigator will interview separately all witnesses nominated by both parties.

5   The next step is the assessment of the evidence. In this regard, the following should be borne in mind by the external counsellor who is conducting the investigation. However, if you are conducting the investigation internally, the points apply equally.

   (a) The investigation is about reasonable belief that an incident or incidents took place.

   (b) Consider the impact of the behaviour on all concerned.

   (c) Make sure there is consistency of approach – i.e., all parties should be treated in the same way.

   (d) Pay attention to the witnesses' statements – e.g., whether they are offering evidence to support or negate the complaint.

   (e) Any admission by the accused.

   (f) The behaviour of all parties following the incident – e.g., did the victim rush out in tears; did the accused turn to witnesses and suggest the victim overreacted; was there any further victimisation inside or outside the organisation?

   (g) It is not relevant how the alleged perpetrator treated you in the course of the interview.

The interviews

1   Stress why the interviews are taking place under the company's harassment and bullying policy.

2   Explain their rights of representation or accompaniment – different companies have different policies on this. Some allow only a union member or member of staff whereas others permit someone from outside to attend. You need to make it clear that anyone accompanying the person being interviewed does not speak and is there to offer support only.

3   Have a manager or someone from the management team present.

4   Explain that written notes will be made of the interview and only the relevant people will have access to them.
5   Stress that the proceedings are confidential and, aside from those people who 'need to know', this interview will not be common knowledge throughout the organisation.
6   Make clear that the organisation will do everything possible to prevent victimisation of its employees.
7   Explain that it is your role to establish the facts and the importance of their contribution in enabling you to do this.
8   Don't make judgements about the person being complained about until a thorough investigation has been carried out and you have seen and heard all the evidence available.
9   Ask direct questions relating directly to the written complaint.
10   You cannot answer questions like 'What will happen to X?' In the first place, you will have no idea, and, in the second, it is not your role to give out information.
11   Thank the interviewees for their contributions.

All interviews should follow the same format whether with the victim(s), alleged perpetrator(s) or witness(es).

The report

The report is written according to the original brief. The investigator's role is not to make decisions about disciplinary procedures and related matters.

1   Summarise the allegations you have been asked to address.
2   State clearly who you interviewed and when.
3   Outline the findings for each allegation
    (a) summarise the response to each allegation and its impact on every person interviewed;
    (b) remain open-minded and fair throughout – your findings should contain no value judgements.
4   Repeat process for each allegation.
5   Refer back to the organisation's own policy.
6   Be aware that other evidence could be collected about other instances or in support of either side. Do not include issues of job performance or examples of good or bad character references; these are not relevant to the investigation.

7 Remember that if witnesses are unwilling to come forward and speak it does not necessarily follow that the alleged incident/s did not happen. It may mean that people are too scared to or they simply do not want to get involved.

8 Conclusions: write a summary of the findings and why they do, or do not, contravene the company policy.

9 Recommendations: the investigator should make only those recommendations that are within either their remit from the organisation or appropriate under the circumstances. Examples of recommendations that might be made are:

(a) Constructive resolutions such as counselling or mediation.

(b) Professional development for either or both parties.

(c) Management skills training.

(d) A mentor system to enable personal coaching to take place.

The investigator's role is not to make recommendations as to the course of disciplinary action, or indeed if any should be taken. This decision is left to management. In some cases, the perpetrator is genuinely shocked at the impact of their behaviour and all that is necessary is an informal warning and an apology.

Be prepared to attend the board of management meeting if this was agreed at the brief-taking stage.

In some instances the investigator's role is over once the report is handed in. You need to remember that as the investigator, even if you found that the perpetrator had grossly contravened the company policy on dignity at work, you do not have the right to know the outcome of any disciplinary action.

Once the investigation has been completed, the investigator cannot work as a counsellor or mediator to any of the people involved since this would lead to role conflict.

Some cases can be emotionally distressing; therefore be prepared to debrief with another investigator, your supervisor or other skilled professional and do not be tempted to gossip to anyone within the organisation.

After the investigation: suggestions for managers

1 Read the report.

2 Take into account any previous complaints against them.

3   Take into account any evidence about the impact of the behaviour on the person making a complaint, e.g., deteriorating work performance or absenteeism.

4   On occasions an alleged harasser will admit to the incident on the grounds that they did not deliberately cause offence. In these cases, an informal warning, an apology to all concerned and an agreement from management to monitor the situation may be all that is needed to bring this unwelcome issue to an end.

5   Remember that admissions are not necessary to take disciplinary action, since witnesses may be too afraid to come forward. The more serious the incident, the less likely it is that it will be supported by either an admission or witness statement.

6   Take appropriate disciplinary action in line with the organisation's grievance procedure.

Please also see Chapter 14 of this manual for further practical considerations relating to the counsellor/psychologist who is planning to transfer their skills to organisational investigations.

Chapter 8

Mediation

Mediation is the process of assisting people to find a common solution to a common problem. The mediator is an objective facilitator whose aim is to enable people in conflict to reach their own solutions with a win/win outcome.

Doherty (1998) defines mediation as follows: 'To intervene between parties in order to reconcile them.' This technique has been used with great success for many years to settle disputes between nations. It is now being used increasingly in the workplace.

Evarts *et al.* (1983) expand on this definition when they describe mediation as the intervention of a neutral third party who: 'assists the parties at dispute in finding their own way out of the dispute through equity and consensus'.

The parties attending mediation have the same aim: to change the situation they are in. Mediation offers each party the opportunity to be heard in private by the mediator and then an opportunity to be heard by the other side. Once both sides have stated their case, the process of negotiation begins in order to find ways for each side to get some of what they want and so enable them to move forward.

Mediation is a future-focused, voluntary process that can bring about a solution to not only the disputants' distress, but also the stresses of their managers, the Human Resources department, and any others who may become involved in the conflict. As a result, mediation can minimise the costs of lost productivity, and avoid the disruptions and expense of tribunals and litigation.

The advantages of mediation

Although mediation is not a panacea for all conflicts and all situations, as a method for resolving issues arising from workplace bullying it offers some compelling advantages:

- All parties in the dispute have equal power. They are all given the space to speak and be heard, listen, reflect on their own values and exchange their views.
- The parties themselves negotiate and participate fully in making decisions about their own lives and what is right for them.
- Because the result being aimed for is a win/win situation, the parties retain their dignity throughout. In addition, the untenable situation for the loser in a win/lose outcome is avoided.
- The process is constructive and informal, with a simple step-by-step structure.
- The procedures are aimed equally at all levels of the hierarchy.
- Mediation is confidential.
- The facilitator is an impartial person with no investment in the outcome of the mediation and can therefore facilitate the process while remaining neutral. This avoids the possibility of any role conflict and any accusation of bias for or against either side.
- Mediation can be used to change disputing behaviour and other destructive behaviour patterns.

Doherty (1998) sees mediation as a useful tool when an organisation is going through a process of change, such as when launching a new or updated Dignity at Work policy. Mediation can help in managing these changes, creating better working relationships, and providing an outlet for people to communicate with each other during this cultural shift. If staff at all levels in an organisation feel that they can have their views heard, they are less likely to suffer stress and respond to that with absenteeism.

When is mediation indicated?

Most people are not happy being in dispute with their colleagues or managers – whether one is bullying or harassing another, whether one is a witness to another's inappropriate behaviour, or whether one is the victim of another's bullying. In general, people want to go to work, get along with their colleagues, be treated well and receive a fair remuneration for what they do. Mediation can help organisations satisfy these basic desires and sustain a contented workforce by resolving conflict and making possible realistic, workable agreements.

Situations in which mediation is an appropriate way forward include:

- when the conflict is between manager and staff member,
- when the conflict is between peers,
- when all parties are willing to attend voluntarily,
- when the problem is equally balanced,
- where it is important to maintain relationships,
- when it is early in the process of the conflict,
- where there is a history of good relationships in the past,
- when the parties are willing to keep the process confidential,
- where all parties involved want to remain in control of the outcome,
- where the issues are solvable,
- where the parties need the space to let off steam and then move on, and
- where neither party sees this as a form of revenge on the other.

When is mediation not indicated?

Not all situations can be successfully mediated. Consultants should therefore ensure, before undertaking each case, that they are in possession of all the relevant facts so that they can make an objective and rational assessment of whether mediation is the correct approach in the circumstances.

Contra-indicators for mediation:

- One person is intimidated and afraid of the other person.
- One person is refusing to communicate or is not attending voluntarily.
- Threats of physical violence.
- Threats of emotional abuse.
- Power imbalance.
- Long history of entrenched attitudes.
- Previous attempts at mediation failed.

- One or both parties has/have issues with drugs, alcohol or mental health.
- Criminal legal action is underway.
- A legal or tribunal decision has already been handed down on the same issue.
- One or both parties is/are not competent to negotiate.

The above contra-indicators pertain to the people involved in the conflict. From the point of view of the consultant, there is another contra-indicator: where, for instance, the issue is too close and triggers things too personal to allow the required impartiality. For example, if you are asked to work in an area where you have already taken sides on hearing the story as told by a third person, save yourself the distress and stress of dealing with it by not accepting the case.

Although an integral part of being professional is being able to identify and separate out what are our own issues, if something elicits an extreme reaction from us it is better to hand it over to a colleague.

Skills and qualities of the mediator

Many of the qualities and skills needed by a mediator are those used by psychologists and counsellors in their work. The mediation process is similar to that used when working with couples who are in dispute. The key to working as a mediator is thus being able to transfer those skills that are appropriate but leaving out others that might hinder or disrupt the mediation process. For example, the mediator should be careful not to make any gestures such as nodding as this might be misconstrued by the parties as agreement. Mediators must guard against doing anything that might create the impression of anything less than impartiality.

The specific skills needed to be a mediator are:

- *Active listening* – giving people the space to say what they need to say and allowing them to be angry and upset; asking appropriate and encouraging questions to enable the facts to emerge and be gathered effectively; feeding back accurately.
- *Summarising* – the ability to gather and re-present the facts, feelings and issues accurately.

- *Building rapport* – presenting yourself as a professional person who takes the issues seriously; creating an atmosphere in which people feel that their thoughts and feelings are understood; giving the disputants a chance to make their own decisions at their own pace; demonstrating a real interest in helping the parties resolve their dispute.
- *Assertiveness* – being able to present your role and needs in the process clearly whilst respecting the disputants and not putting them down; being prepared to establish ground rules and willing to intervene if these are not adhered to (for example, intervening firmly but fairly if one party interrupts the other when it is not their turn to speak).
- *Facilitation* – assisting the parties in communicating, listening, and expressing facts, emotions and concerns.
- *Problem-solving* – finding the facts, identifying the problems and clarifying solutions by working out step-by-step plans of action with the disputants.
- *Conflict management* – staying calm, not taking material personally, remaining assertive, encouraging communication between the parties even when emotions are running high, defusing anger, suggesting 'cool-down' breaks. It is important to acknowledge and respond to the strong feelings that are generated and not ignore them. And, through all this, remembering to keep positive.
- *Presentation skills* – communicating ideas in direct and simple ways (for instance, by avoiding jargon) so that everyone in the group can understand. Recognising the potency of your own verbal expression, body language and gestures in communicating with the parties, and using these appropriately.
- *Management of the mediation process* – combining a variety of skills to provide a safe structure for all parties by keeping control of the process.

The specific qualities needed to be a mediator are:

- *Understanding people and situations* – experience in working with people and their different behaviours.
- *Ability to learn from experience* – capacity to build on knowledge, self-awareness and an awareness of others.
- *Genuineness* – honesty and an awareness of one's own strengths and weaknesses.

- *Acceptance* – a willingness to truly accept others, even those finding it difficult to move out of their entrenched positions.
- *Respect* – understanding and valuing differences, and being aware of personal prejudices.
- *Impartiality* – a concern for the outcome for both sides and an ability to demonstrate this to them.
- *Self-awareness* – paying attention to one's own feelings and behaviour so as not to treat the parties unfairly without realising it.
- *Flexibility* – the ability to change the process in order to meet the needs of each situation.
- *Commitment to equal opportunities* – understanding how issues such as racism, ageism and sexism play a part in disputes between people, being aware of different cultural needs, and being able to work with a diversity of people in a non-discriminatory way.
- *Analytical ability* – the aptitude to assess the realistic chances of change and agreement, monitoring this throughout the process, and knowing when to stop and when to continue.
- *Creativity* – the ability to come up with ideas, to try different ways of working where necessary, and be adaptable to changing situations.
- *Professionalism* – taking the work seriously and being prepared to devote as much time as is necessary.

The process

The following are, in general, the steps in the mediation process. In practice, some may not apply to specific cases while in others some steps should be combined.

1   Listen to what the organisation is expecting the mediation to achieve, get a sense of the organisational culture and what the issues are. Make a decision on whether the issues are appropriate for mediation. Establish that all parties are attending the process voluntarily.

2   Agree the contract with the organisation and establish where the interviews are to take place. Specify that it must be away from the main open-plan office so that you will be neither disturbed nor observed by people passing by (a glass-fronted office is obviously not appropriate). Unlike counselling, mediation

normally takes place around a table so you will need a desk or table and the appropriate number of chairs. Check ahead whether water, tissues, tea, coffee, etc. will be available. Discuss when the process is to take place, how much time will be needed, and your fees. Discuss who will be making the appointments and other administrative arrangements with the people concerned (will it be a member of the support team or you?).

3   Introduce yourself and your role and explain the confidential nature of the process to each person involved. Interview people individually, allowing them to tell their story. Employ active listening skills of feedback and clarifying questions to make sure that you have understood what they are saying. Through questioning, identify and verbalise what you consider to be the underlying issues. People often claim to be upset about something when, in fact, something else is the major sticking point. Finding the real, core issue at this stage can help to reach a lasting outcome. Be prepared to deal with strong emotions like anger, frustration, fear or hopelessness. For a process to reach this stage people have usually been hurt or angered in some way and this is the place for these emotions to be aired. Find out what the parties are hoping to achieve from the process and if they have any views on how this achievement can be realised. Allow sufficient time for people to tell their story, but without repeating themselves.

4   Allow yourself some time to think through the stories that you have heard and prepare yourself to put the parties together to help them make decisions about a way forward. Remind yourself to remain impartial and professional and put aside any issues of your own.

5   Bring the parties together, welcome them, thank them for coming voluntarily and explain the purpose of the meeting. Explain that mediation is 'non-binding' and 'without prejudice' and that you cannot be called upon at a later date to give evidence anywhere else. However, do explain that it can have positive results if all parties are willing to work together towards a common goal.

6   Establish the ground rules:
    •   everyone is required to show respect to one another, including the mediator;

- everyone will be given an opportunity to speak;
- language that either other person finds offensive must not be used;
- everyone should be allowed to say what they have to say without interruption;
- people must speak to each other and not through someone else;
- emphasise that the purpose of the meeting is to try and come to some agreement;
- remind them that you are the facilitator;
- any outcome will be based on their negotiations and decisions;
- the agreements will be written down;
- reiterate that the process is confidential – it is not to be taken outside the room or outside the organisation.

These ground rules are established to prevent a situation where people sit or stand and shout at each other. It also makes it easier for the mediator to intervene (e.g., 'Do you recall that at the beginning you agreed not to interrupt?'), The ground rules mark a beginning stage of disputants' agreeing on something – thus setting a precedent for working together.

7   Establish what all parties hope to achieve from this meeting.

8   Allow each side to repeat their story.

9   Be prepared to be directive to ensure that each party sticks to the ground rules.

10   Help them to identify the problem.

11   After each person has said their piece, feed it back to all parties in an emotionally neutral and non-judgemental way. Identify the main issues and feelings. Check with the owner of the story that you have understood it correctly.

12   Encourage the parties to express the effect that the situation is having on them and to communicate these feelings to all concerned.

13   Be prepared to deal with a wide variety of reactions and feelings from the other side. Remember that, in the context of bullying, this may be the first time the bully has heard about the effect of their behaviour on the other party. Bear in mind how the victim might be feeling in the presence of the bully.

14 Creatively help them to brainstorm, identify solutions and think of ways, acceptable to all, that could move the process forward. Never rush this process.

15 Once oral agreements have been made, check that the parties have the authority to carry them through. An agreement that needs a third person's permission is not an agreement. When this has been established, have the agreements reduced to writing and invite all parties to sign and take a copy with them. Include, as one of the points of agreement, an undertaking to keep the entire matter confidential.

16 Thank everyone for attending and taking an active part in the process.

Depending on your contract with the organisation, it may be appropriate for you to call all parties after a month and see how the agreement is working. If you intend to do this, inform all parties of your intention before they depart.

Of course, despite the best efforts of the mediator and one or both sides, mediation may not always produce the desired results. Nevertheless, it will still have given people an opportunity to let the other people know their views and be heard. In cases of minor complaints of bullying or harassment, it also gives the perpetrator an opportunity to understand the impact of their behaviour on others and make the appropriate changes.

Finally, a quote on mediation from Doherty (in personal conversation, 1999) that resonated with me is that mediation is about 'bringing people to their senses and not to their knees'.

Comparisons with other methods

Conciliation

There is sometimes confusion between the terms *conciliation* and *mediation*. *Conciliation* is used by ACAS (Advisory, Conciliation and Arbitration Service) to refer to a process essentially the same as *mediation* as described both here and as most other organisations use the term. ACAS mediation makes formal, though non-binding, recommendations which are intended to provide a basis for settling a dispute.

Conciliation, like mediation, involves a third party who helps people to negotiate with each other. Conciliators offer the parties advice as well as possible solutions to their problems, whereas mediation is, as we have seen, a voluntary process designed to enable the disputants themselves to decide the solutions to their problems.

Arbitration

Arbitration is an older method of conflict resolution within organisations. *Black's Law Dictionary* (5th edn, 1983) defines arbitration as the employment of an impartial third person who has the voluntary agreement of all parties to resolve the dispute. 'The arbitrator, a neutral person, presides at the hearing, hears all the facts and evidence of the parties and thereafter renders an award which is final and binding.'

Arbitration is judgement-based and results in a winner and a loser, while a mediator, without coercive powers, has as their sole aim the construction of an equitable settlement based on consensus (i.e., a win/win outcome for all concerned).

A mediator has no coercive powers and their only goal is the construction of an equitable settlement based on consensus. An arbitrator, on the other hand, is obliged to reach a decision based on legal principles.

The agreement reached in the mediation process is not legally binding. However, a memorandum committed to writing and signed by both parties adds power to the process by restoring dignity to the individuals themselves who do not feel that they have had the authority of others forced upon them.

Grievance and disciplinary procedures

Reynolds (2000) believes that the more traditionally used grievance and disciplinary procedures do not compare favourably with mediation because the underlying disputes are often left unresolved. Often, the dispute may appear to have been settled, but in the aftermath one of the parties leaves the organisation, asks for a transfer or holds onto the resentment. This held-onto resentment inevitably develops into a new dispute later on. Reynolds, himself an experienced mediator, therefore regards mediation as useful to organisations because of both interpersonal and cost benefits. In their research on local government, Findlay and Reynolds (1997) found that actual 'hard' costs were reduced by two-thirds using mediation instead of traditional grievance procedures.

Chapter 9

Conclusions

Where we stand now

August 2001 saw the UK government providing funding of £1.5 million for innovative projects in the workplace.

Companies championing schemes to crack down on bullying at work, to build better work/life balance practices and to resolve disputes are among those that received a boost from the DTI. Talking of the scheme, in a press release issued by Department of Trade and Industry on 7 August 2001, Employment Minister Alan Johnson said:

> The dark days when management was by coercion and negotiation by threat may seem like the distant past, but we must continue to improve. Today's successful company realises the full potential of its most important resource – its people – by ensuring they are equipped to perform at their best and listening to their contributions.

If only Alan Johnson were right. The organisations that are applying for grants under this scheme are run by people who are already aware of what bullying is and that it is happening inside their organisations. These are not the people who need educating – it is the organisations run by people who believe 'it doesn't happen here', or 'bullying is just the latest fad to capture media attention' that would benefit more.

It is easy to understand why people who are being bullied at work in the main leave their employment instead of saying or doing anything about it. However, this doesn't contribute to stopping that behaviour or preventing its happening to someone else.

In an ideal world, people recognise they are being bullied and ask those responsible to stop. If this doesn't have the desired outcome, they go to Human Resources, which deals with it efficiently. The perpetrators learn from the experience and in future treat others appropriately. Organisations are able to live up to their mission statements and all members of staff feel that they are being treated fairly and with respect.

The key to getting to this stage is awareness, both on an organisational and individual level. People need to be self-aware and accept the impact of their behaviour on others, asking themselves 'Am I treating that person fairly?' and 'Is my behaviour appropriate?' They also need to get feedback from trusted others. Supervisors and managers must be trained in recognising bullying behaviour and in taking action to prevent it.

Bassman (1992) stresses that all staff should be trained in the identification of bullying patterns rather than individual incidents. This process would protect both the accused and the accusers and would offer a way of recognising and stopping inappropriate behaviours at an early stage. It may also encourage people to think twice before treating a colleague improperly.

Managers and Human Resources need to be prepared and ready to deal with incidents of bullying as they arise and not bury their heads in the metaphorical sand, hoping that it will go away if they ignore it. Implementing their carefully worded and laid-out policies is time consuming and may mean they have to put the disciplinary procedures into practice. For many people in management, this causes almost as much stress as those being bullied are suffering, especially if they are forced to terminate the employment of someone with dependants who is shouting about their rights and threatening to sue.

It may be easier to ignore complaints in the first instance. However, in the longer term, when someone comes forward to say that bullying behaviour has been going on with the full knowledge of both their manager and the Human Resources department, it is likely to mean a more complex and potentially difficult legal battle later on.

Also, from a moral and human perspective, how as a manager would you feel about yourself if you were accused of colluding and even condoning bullying behaviours that result in serious stress-related illness to one or more members of your staff?

The way forward

Coyne *et al.* (2000), speaking for the TUC at the BPS Annual Occupational Conference, stated that five million people are estimated to be bullied at work at some point in their lives and every office has someone who is a victim of workplace bullying. His research suggests that there are personality types who are more likely to be victims of bullying and who can be helped by counselling or assertiveness training before they are bullied. On the other hand, I argue that this seems to place the onus on people themselves to prevent their being bullied rather than training their colleagues, with the potential to bully, to stop

Research data, newspapers, and personal experience encourage us to acknowledge that bullying is alive and well in our places of work and no longer allow us to revel in the smugness of 'It doesn't happen in this organisation'.

Hoel and Cooper (2000) suggest that the way forward to create a culture free from bullying is to introduce effective, safe and fair policies. Policies need to be safe in that they protect people as far as possible from retribution. They further suggest that in order for policies to be effective a monitoring system needs to be put in place.

Hoel and Cooper (2000) further suggest the challenging and confrontation of abusive and bullying management styles. In their UMIST study they found that these 'confrontational' and 'macho' management styles are linked to negative organisational outcomes. They recommend instead that organisations encourage co-operative styles of management.

They also suggest that any risk-assessment strategy carried out within organisations focusing on psychosocial work hazards should include bullying and victimisation, which is a move towards reducing stress at work.

Secondly, we all need to ask ourselves 'Am I a perpetrator of bullying behaviours, no matter how subtle? Do I manipulate to get my own way? Do I take the praise for ideas or work that are not mine? Do I always treat others either with dignity or respect? Do I shout or snap when I am under stress, tired or distressed? Do I stop and think what impact my behaviour might be having on other people?'

Once we, as professionals working in the field, are aware of the effect of our own behaviour, and we have an awareness of what bullying is, then it is our duty to educate others, and bring in consultants to help write training programmes and policies.

In line with the thinking of Hoel and Cooper (2000) it is not enough to identify the likely and actual perpetrators of bullying behaviours. We need to be working towards creating a whole system with a non-bullying ethos.

Further, we should read all the excellent materials available, in print or on the web. Please refer to Appendix II, 'Useful Information', for a listing.

Make the training programmes and the launching or relaunching of the policy an important event in your organisational calendar, and attendance at the workshops and seminars compulsory for all staff, no matter how junior or senior. If senior management and HR are seen to be taking it seriously, the better is the possibility that the rest of the organisation will do so too.

Educate the managers. Doing the job in the same manner as they have done for the last 15 years and getting good results is no longer acceptable if managers are bullying the staff to achieve it. Make management training programmes a part of the assessment process and, consequently, not optional.

This view is confirmed by Rayner *et al.* (2002) who acknowledge the increasing demands being made on people working in cultures where diversity and bullying are issues still in the process of being dealt with. In today's business world, employers need staff of the highest quality to remain competitive while employees are demanding decent treatment in return. Rayner *et al.* therefore suggest that management training needs to reflect the realities and pressures that managers are facing at present as well as those likely in the future.

One way of achieving this is to introduce awareness programmes that invite people to look at their own behaviours and ask themselves questions such as 'Am I a bully; am I guilty of inappropriate behaviour?' If people conclude that they do fall into this category, they have the option of stopping the offending behaviour. They should also be made aware of the consequences of not doing so. For many people, being able to identify the effect of their behaviour on others is sufficient to make them want to stop or seek help in stopping.

This approach is preferable to one in which the bully is demonised, where the effect might be that instead of people owning their own behaviours – and understanding the desirability of changing them – they become defensive or enter a state of denial: 'No, no, that characterisation isn't me . . . I'm not that bad.' By being introduced to the gentler concept of negative behaviours people are more disposed to admit to it and do something about it.

Just as, on an individual level, people should take responsibility for their own behaviours and how these affect others, so organisations also need to take responsibility by not colluding with behaviours that either create a bullying culture or allow one to flourish unchecked. If staff cut-backs have been made with the result that a few people are striving harder and harder to meet unrealistic deadlines, the unintended effect might be that these people are being set up to fail and the foundations of a bullying culture are being laid. By moving away from finger-pointing towards a spirit of teamwork and joint effort, a culture of dignity and respect, where people can feel valued and motivated, is created instead. The knock-on effect for the organisation is that people stay in their jobs, the business as a whole does not have to face the costs of recruiting and training new staff, and costly litigation is avoided.

This view is supported by Rigby (2002) who regards bullying as an indictment of the system and finds the solution to bullying at work to be in replacing old, bad systems with new, good ones.

More than anything else, I believe that professionals need both to acknowledge when bullying is going on within their organisations and, moreover, understand that doing nothing to end it is collusion.

Achieving an organisation in which dignity and fairness for all is the norm is not easy. However, remember that outside of your organisation are people with the skills to help you write and implement policies and to train your workers to understand that in order to achieve a fair, safe and happy working environment it needs every individual's contribution.

The MSF General Secretary, Roger Lyons, in October 2001, commented in a press release as follows on a severe sexual harassment case: 'To all those employers who believe they can bully and harass their staff with impunity I send this message: We will not give up the chase until justice is done.'

Part 2 of this manual is addressed to counsellors and psychologists who are either already working – or who wish to work – with organisations that need help in introducing, implementing and maintaining their Dignity at Work policies.

Part 2

The role of counsellors/ psychologists in organisations

Many psychologists and counsellors who have not had the experience of working in organisations may have some apprehensions about making the transition from private practice or public-service employment.

This part of the book is designed to offer useful information to help you transfer the skills you already have, through your training and experience, and apply them to working within organisations.

Counsellors and psychologists can take many varied and useful roles in organisations:

- Counselling – either as an internal or external provider.
- Training – in harassment and bullying awareness.
- Consultancy – writing and launching policies.
- Team building.
- Harassment investigation – being the external objective professional who can carry out this task within the guidelines of the company policy and avoiding role conflict within the organisation.
- Mediation – offering the organisation a cost-effective and less stressful way for all parties to resolve conflict.
- Professional development, mentoring and coaching – working with any of the parties concerned to move on from the events and, for some, to facilitate behaviour change. For those found guilty of bullying, it may involve working with them to fulfil their new objectives.

Chapter 10

The role of counsellors/ psychologists in organisations

Why use counsellors/psychologists

Many counselling and psychotherapy trainings view the role of the counsellor/psychotherapist in the context of one client and one counsellor within a closed unit. Counselling in organisations requires that the counsellor sees the client in terms of a much bigger system. It is not just about the organisation sending a stressed employee over to the counsellor and washing their hands of any responsibility until the client is well and can return. There are steps beyond that simplistic scenario: allowing the client to return to work without any other changes having taken place is most likely to result in the client soon also returning to the same state they were in when they needed help. This is not good for the client. It is also a situation that will make the employer vulnerable to litigation, which is obviously not good for the company.

Another compelling reason for using outside counsellors is the avoidance of role conflict. It occurs in situations such as when Human Resources personnel are expected both to break the news about job losses to people who are retrenched or otherwise terminated and to act as counsellors to the distressed. Similarly, it would also constitute role conflict to expect them to be harassment investigators and mediators, and also assume responsibility for administering the company's discipline policy.

Transferable skills

In addition to being a counselling psychologist, I am an integrative psychotherapist working within humanistic concepts and with a background in both Transactional Analysis and Gestalt psycho-therapy. I have transferred these learnt skills to working in organisations.

I refer to transferring the skills of being a psychotherapist to working as a consultant within organisations as 'soft skills'. These are the skills we, as trained counsellors/psychotherapists or counselling psychologists, have a tendency to take for granted. Yet they are the essentials for working in all aspects of organisational consultancy. I have called these skills 'soft' – to differentiate them from fact-based skills such as computer operating or answering factual enquiries – but I think of them as powerful skills. There is nothing soft about knowing who you are, the impact your behaviours have on other people and being willing to change if your behaviour is inappropriate. I believe that it takes a strong person to be able to say 'I got it wrong, my behaviour was inappropriate. I am willing to change and do something about it in order to prevent a similar thing happening to someone else at my hands.'

There are several schools of psychotherapy that I find valuable for organisational work. My particular brand of integration encompasses elements of Gestalt, Family Systems, Transactional Analysis (TA) and Emotional Intelligence. These theories, parti-cularly TA, have given me my core structure for the way I see the world, run my life and consequently work as an organisational psychologist. TA is a thread that runs through my thinking and forms the basis on which I view organisations. I see bullying within organisations as growing out of a bullying culture.

As a basis for my work, I use Rogers's core conditions of congruence, unconditional positive regard and empathy (Rogers 1961). I find that they provide me with a constant personal gauge by which to monitor my own behaviour.

I treat each side with respect and I actively listen to what they have to say. My TA training has taught me to recognise games and rackets, which I cut across and teach alternative ways of com-municating by modelling and reframing (Schiff et al., 1975), and emotional literacy (Steiner, 1984).

Thinking in terms of working as an organisational consultant a client-centred approach can be useful. Cockman et al. (1998) propose a useful methodology, the consulting cycle, which offers guidelines for beginning a process. The following material is adapted from their work.

- Begin the initial contact and establish a working relationship. Model dignity and respect for the client and expect to be treated in the same way (allowing no other alternative).
- Contracting – find out what the client's needs are and state your own.
- Collecting the data – finding out about the issue/s.
- Diagnosing the problem – by making sense of the data.
- Generating options – make decisions as part of a consultation process with the client, and decide the way forward.
- Implementing the plans and taking action.
- Disengaging – arranging any necessary follow-up action.

By organising and planning the work and deciding on an approximate time scale, the consultant avoids a situation in which they are left feeling resentful that the client seems to be wanting more and more of them for a fee that has been fixed in advance. Make sure the client understands the amount of time you are prepared to give to the work, what input you will want from them, and what support you will require from the organisation (e.g., secretarial support etc.).

In the early stages, do not take on work that you feel anxious about. If you are not certain about what might be entailed in particular engagements, discuss it first with your supervisor and check whether they will be able to facilitate the work from behind the scenes.

The following are some of the transferable skills by which counsellors/psychologists add value to their work in organisations.

Listening skills

- Active listening.
- Questioning.
- Probing.
- Summarising.
- Note-taking.
- Empathy.
- Unconditional respect (i.e., respecting someone for being a human being and not making judgements based on what they have been accused of).

Interpersonal skills

Those with well-developed interpersonal skills can deal with people from all levels within the organisation and are able to step into and understand their frame of reference.

Respectful inquiry

One skill the consultant needs to develop is that of inquiry. Erskine (1999) believes that respect for the client is the basis of therapeutic inquiry. This skill should be transferred into the consultant/ organisational client relationship.

It is the respect demonstrated by the consultant that enables the client to feel safe and discuss what are often delicate organisational issues. Without respect, inquiry can feel invasive and interrogatory. As with therapeutic clients, we may not necessarily like the people we are dealing with, but we need to respect them as human beings who have their own values and opinions. However, respect does not mean simply agreeing with them; a consultant is employed to help the organisation as a whole as well as the individuals within that organisation. This may mean recommending changes that on the surface are unpalatable.

Genuine interest

Another transferable skill from our clinical practice is genuine interest. This we demonstrate in an organisational setting in the same way as in a clinical setting. It is our non-verbal communication, our tone of voice, the way in which we greet people. Do we smile and look genuinely pleased to see them?

A genuine interest in the work setting will enable us to work at an in-depth level of understanding from which we can help the client. Genuine interest can be seen as a natural outgrowth of respect.

Although not working as a therapist to the MD or HR personnel who have called you in, using our therapeutic skills in the relationship can be of benefit.

Attunement

Erskine's (1999) concept of attunement is invaluable. He suggests that attunement goes beyond empathy 'Because it involves the deeply personal response of the hearer as well as the intent of the speaker.' The client needs to feel 'understood'. They need to know that the consultant appreciates that they have a problem, understands it and will help in planning the way forward.

As consultants, being attuned to the person in the organisation who instructs us enables us to take a step back and consider how they themselves may be contributing – either positively or negatively – to the issues and what roles they themselves may be taking within them. For example, an HR director who has made herself unapproachable may be surprised to learn that she has been oblivious to a bullying culture because people are afraid to approach her.

As a consultant with the skills to take people on a regressive journey into their own inner psychological world, we need to keep in mind that the scope and extent of our assignment is such that we do not take clients too deeply into areas we are not contracted to work in. We need to bear in mind that we are consultants and not psychotherapists.

Professionalism and commitment

Erskine (1999) talks about professionalism and commitment as forming the basis of the therapeutic relationship. I consider that these same qualities form the basis of a good consultancy relationship. Our professionalism provides both structure and direction for our commitment. It is constructed of knowledge skills and values, which enable us to relate to the organisational client appropriately. Professionalism also means self-monitoring, which enables us to have authentic relationships with people whilst keeping out personal issues.

Part of our being professional includes:

- Dressing in a manner appropriate to the organisation.
- Respecting the organisation's rules, e.g., in a non-smoking building, not smoking.
- Not being seen in the local pub with management even after the investigation/mediation is over. Other people involved may feel uncomfortable and possibly paranoid that their case is being discussed.

Our key resource for working in organisations as a psychologist/ counsellor is ourselves. Consequently, we need to think about the impact we have on other people. Do I use 'therapy speak' which will leave some finance houses in the City recoiling as they fantasise that we will want them to do 'touchy-feely things' and make fools of themselves. Is my language clear and concise? Am I using 'I' statements to instil confidence in my employers so that they feel they can trust me to do the job?

We need to ask ourselves if we look right. We are stepping into the world of organisations out of choice. However, they are not coming to us for counselling and psychotherapy and stepping into our worlds out of choice. You are likely to feel more comfortable if you wear appropriate clothes and gear your appearance so that you fit into the look and feel of the organisation. Of course, since some organisations now have either a dress-down culture or a dress-down day on Fridays, I compromise by wearing a tee-shirt under a suit instead of a formal top as I would feel unprofessional dressed like a vagrant to conform with some of the staff norms!

One very positive way that we as health professionals can demonstrate our value to organisations is by modelling the desired behaviour and attitudes. For example, we must present ourselves in such a way that we warrant respect for our clear thinking and our emotional literacy.

Objectivity

The ability to be demonstratively objective and impartial means that we will not find ourselves in a position where our professionalism could be questioned. This includes:

- Not being tempted to join in office gossip.
- Not being drawn into discussing the case outside of the presentation, even once it has been completed.
- Having the capacity to assess complex direct and indirect evidence in an impartial manner.

Involvement

If the client comes to you at the stage where they are still undecided whether to take formal action you should go through the company's policy with them, help them to understand the terms as laid down, and discuss what will happen should they decide to take the formal route.

Facilitate a process whereby the individual is able to make the decision for themselves. You cannot make it for them even if you find yourself full of self-righteous indignation. Deal with this outside with peers or your supervisor.

An interview, no matter how carefully done, can be destructive for some people. They may not be ready to deal with the situation and all the issues that it may bring up for them from the past.

As an organisational counsellor you are likely to have a time-limited contract – frequently six sessions. Work within the constraints and boundaries of the contract. Know when to refer a client on for longer-term treatment.

Giving information

Many people who have been bullied blame themselves. 'It must be something I have done – he doesn't bully anyone else.' Giving information as to how bullies frequently operate within organisations can help people to understand.

Normalisation

Like many clients who seek therapy for other issues, people who have been bullied often have a great sense of shame. Normalising these feelings of shame can be an important part of our work.

Erskine (1999) considers normalisation to be 'A way of countering these self-derogatory beliefs and help clients to realise that their behaviours and internal experiences are normal and predictable responses to their life situation, environment and their genetic make-up.'

Chapter 11

Useful theories

Some theories of counselling and psychotherapy offer themselves as being highly appropriate to thinking organisationally. In this chapter I highlight the four that I have drawn on most in formulating my approach to working in organisations.

A systems perspective

Seeing an organisation in terms of a systems perspective is an easy concept for the consultant to both grasp and translate into acceptable language for the client. Carroll (1997) speaks of being part of the system and also external to it, 'independent yet integrated'. What this implies for the consultant is an ability to offer a service objectively while at the same time understanding the system from which the rupture has emerged.

Morgan (1986) offers a systems approach to understanding organisations:

1   The organisation does not exist in a vacuum; it is part of, and related to, the environment.
2   The organisation comprises a number of interrelated sub-systems.
3   The organisation, to flourish, needs an internal congruency between its sub-systems.

Morgan suggests further that the organisational culture represents the 'unconscious' of the organisation.

According to Campbell *et al.* (1994), systems thinking does not explain why people and organisations behave the way they do. Instead, it offers a framework for understanding the world according to its many interrelated parts. Systems thinking is thus concerned with the whole rather than the individual components. Behaviour is seen as a response to the system. Therefore, bullying within an organisation can take place only if the system colludes with it. Peltier (2001) considers that a person's behaviour may be a 'manoeuvre to influence or protect the system or a reaction to organisational stressors'.

As human beings we respond to the events going on around us and narrow our perspective to relate them to ourselves. We look for external events and factors that are 'responsible' for triggering our response. Campbell *et al.* view systemic thinking as a discipline that offers a framework to observe and understand the complex, multi-layered processes within an organisation. 'The problem is not a problem in itself, but is part of a larger process involving many "other" people, other "behaviours", and "other" meanings.'

This way of thinking about an organisation's problems lays the responsibility for the existence of a negative work culture in the hands of not just the management team but also extends it to everyone who forms part of the system. As an example, a culture of dignity and respect for all will not work if the contracted-out catering department operates within an abusive culture where people are treated badly. This will permeate through into the major part of the organisation, with food being served by unhappy, anxious people who are not being treated well and, in turn, do not treat the people they serve with dignity and respect.

Systemic thinking further gives the individual an opportunity to look at where they fit into the bigger system, what influence they have and what the impact of their behaviour on others is. People can stop and ask themselves what they are doing to contribute to a bullying work culture. Do they communicate with people or just give instructions; do they see themselves working as part of a team for the good of the team or are they focused solely on their own performance review and pay increase? Campbell *et al.* consider that the individual who is trying to secure their own power base without thinking about the consequences for the organisation is acting from a position of insecurity and anxiety. Rumours of job losses, management changes and mergers create this type of anxiety for the individual.

A system is 'a whole greater than the sum of its parts' and if the parts all work together in harmony the organisation is seen to be an efficient, functioning system. Organisations grow and change, with the potential of disrupting and causing disharmony. This can be avoided by acknowledging the change and involving all parts of the system in the adjustment to change by informing the individuals who make up the system. A dictate from above proclaiming 'we now operate a culture of dignity and respect' will not work! However, involving representatives from each sector of the system – the shop floor, the unions, the various levels of management and the senior management team – needs to be part of the discussions and negotiations in the preparation for change.

I have found the thinking of Peltier (2001) on systems (as applied to coaching) not only extremely useful but, in addition, relevant to organisational consultancy.

Here and now – a systems approach to consultancy focuses on the here and now: the position at the moment. Historical reasons explaining how the organisation, department or team got to this point are not relevant. So, for instance, when you are told that the culture is based on what was created by the long-since-retired founder who had an autocratic leadership style, this is 'information overload' – and quite beside the point.

Process – taking a systems approach when looking at the culture of an organisation we think in terms of process rather than content. How do people communicate, what are the acceptable 'norms' of behaviours, do the behaviours change under stress?

When a change takes place in one level it has knock-on effect throughout the rest of the organisation. From a systems perspective we are not looking at the reasons and rationale for and leading up to the changes, we are looking at the facts of the changes. For example, when the Equal Opportunities policy was launched what happened in the organisation?

Problem locus – the problem locus is based on the concept in family systems of one individual manifesting the 'symptoms' of the family. When applied to organisations, one person or group of people carry the 'blame' for the whole system. In order for individuals to change within a system the whole system needs to change as they are interrelated. For example, dismissing a persistent bully within an organisation may be a short-term solution because the bully would have modelled their behaviours to others and, if the system doesn't change to exclude the possibility of bullying behaviour taking root, old patterns will be repeated. In a similar vein, Lane (1990) puts forward the view that introducing counselling into a dysfunctional organisation will maintain the level of dysfunction. So, for instance, in an organisation where bullying is rife and people stay away from work to avoid the abuse, counselling to reduce absenteeism and simply 'getting them back to work' is not the answer

As an impartial external consultant employed to work with cultural change in the organisation, you will find that by spending time talking to people and watching how they interrelate, you will get a sense of the rules and norms of the organisation. You will also understand the nature and composition of the real power base: the people who make and break the rules. These are not necessarily the people with the official power.

When an external consultant is able to make observations it gives the client organisation the option of making changes. In preparing them for the consequences of change, consultants will often observe how organisations resist change and try to find ways of pulling the system back to the status quo – the equilibrium they know and understand even though it doesn't work. Recognising this; the consultant must find a way in which changes can be made to maintain stability under stress.

For example, a negative and highly resistant response could result if the organisation were to simply send an e-mail to every member of staff informing them that the organisation has adopted a Dignity at Work policy and that henceforth everyone will adhere to it. This would probably meet with such resistance that people would fight against the policy in such a way that the system would slip back into its old ways of colluding with an environment that supports harassment. Instead, the policy should be launched to groups of individuals in such a way as to answer the questions, reduce the anxieties, and deal with the reservations. Explain to people that this change is not only about them as an individual but also about their behaviour and its consequences within the wider system. Relate this to specifics: it is not OK to treat your immediate work team well and then 'back-bite' another department or blame them when things go wrong.

If people on the management team understand family systems and how each person's role interlinks, then they will understand how they themselves can in effect be working towards maintaining a dysfunctional culture. Only then can the beginnings of change be made.

Transactional Analysis

Of all my training and experience, I feel that TA has given me the most useful tools for working in organisations. A good understanding of ego states and basic transactions allows me to be aware of myself and understand the person who is employing me (in whatever capacity) within the organisation. This enables me to communicate clearly and without hidden agendas on either side. Many people think in terms of what is going wrong in the organisation and then look for the problems. I believe in looking out for what is going right, i.e., what they are doing well, and then 'stroking' people for this. This gives us a positive economy from which to begin working.

I will not attempt to explain this model in detail here as it is eloquently done in many basic TA texts, particularly Stewart and Joines (1987). Instead, I will attempt to explain how I use TA thinking in my work with organisations.

Transactional Analysis is a useful tool for looking at organisations and the many permutations of interpersonal relationships. It provides an elegant and simple language for thinking about what is going on within an organisation. As de Villere (1981) puts it, 'Unless you are a firm believer in the life complication theory, why make difficult things understandable when you can confuse them with jargon and unnecessary analysis?' I prefer to keep it simple.

I looked through the early TA literature for material that could be relevant to bullying at work and found a quote by its founder Eric Berne: 'Rudeness is a mere neglect of etiquette or an exhibition of character familiarity' (Berne, 1963). What might he say now on reading some of the case examples given in this and other texts on bullying at work? It leaves me with questions like 'Has the general behaviour of people within organisations become less polite?', 'Do people show less respect for each other in general?' and 'Are we less tolerant about what is acceptable behaviour?'

The most useful aspect of TA thinking for me is the concept of 'contracting' and this is something I am aware of using every day of my working life. Berne (1966) proposes that there are three aspects to be considered when undertaking a contract: administrative, professional and psychological. He also states that parts of contracts will be oral and not in writing, which means that we need to be aware of all that we agree to because an oral contract is still a contract.

The administrative contract should spell out time, place, venue and responsibilities. This is where any practicalities can be dealt with – i.e., what you as the psychologist/counsellor expect in terms of facilities. This includes office space, use of a telephone, access to photocopying facilities, and so on. Steiner (1984) talks about 'consideration', a term taken from the legal world, with reference to charging a realistic fee for the service to be provided. Cancellation charges need also to be discussed at this stage, as it may be difficult for a consultant to take on other work at short notice if the contract is cancelled. As consultants, you must always keep in mind that you are running a business.

The second part, the professional contract, relates to the agreement with the organisation as to what the psychologist/counsellor is going to do for the organisation. We find out what the organisation is expecting us to do for them. Then we use our experience, knowledge and professional judgement to agree to deliver a service within our competence. This part of the contract is essential to get right to enable all parities to feel good about the service provided. We can endeavour to work with a group of people in the hope of achieving a successful outcome using our mediation skills; however, we cannot make promises that it will work. We can agree to carry out professional development work with someone who has been accused of bullying behaviours for the fifth time, but we cannot guarantee the outcome. As one very senior woman who had had formal warnings about her inappropriate behaviours said to me, 'You are trying to change me from a Bette Davis into a Helena Bonham Carter and it will not work.'

The psychological contract is the most difficult because it is not written down or consciously spoken about. It is based on mutual respect and the idea that everyone has a job to do and that all parties are willing. In terms of harassment investigation, the organisation wants to employ you, you want to be employed. Some of the interviewees may be delighted that you are there as a reminder that the organisation cares enough about them to do something about what is going on. However, other members of staff may not respect you as a professional or as a human being. They may want to manipulate you, lie to you and even bully you. Be prepared that some cases may require that you debrief with your supervisor as they may be stressful and, in the early days, undermine your confidence. Not unlike critical incident debriefing, you may find some of what you hear unpalatable.

Fanita English (1975) was the first person to talk about the three-cornered contract when thinking in terms of training within an organisation. The three corners are the organisation, the trainer and the participants – and it may sometimes seem that the three corners are forces pulling in opposition to each other. This can be stressful for the consultant, especially in cases where they see the participant's complaints as being justified and will therefore find against the organisation, which is paying them. They are also likely to have a contract of confidentiality with the participants while, in terms of the feedback loop into the organisation, they will have a duty to pass on meaningful information.

However, sometimes working as an organisational consultant involves even more than three corners. I frequently work for organisations through other organisations. I invoice the organisation that employs me to consult to a second organisation that employs me to work with their staff. I am aware of the need to remain both professional and loyal to all the parties concerned.

There are some unwritten ethical rules about contracts here. For example, if an organisation has sent you into another organisation as a consultant to do some work, they remain your employers and your initial contract is with the company you invoice. It would be unethical and unprofessional to accept work directly from the second organisation without discussing this with your original employer first.

Another useful TA tool is the concept of psychological games. These are sets of repetitive and unsatisfactory interactions played outside of conscious awareness, which end up with people feeling bad even if satisfied that they were right about something. Any changes within an organisation – especially major ones such as mergers or even new people joining a department – can make people more vulnerable to psychological games. A new manager is particularly vulnerable as they may not yet know how the rules of the culture work. Some organisations run on a positive economy, i.e., people are praised for the work they do well, and negative feedback is discouraged or it meets defended reactions and is pushed back to the deliverer. Other organisations do not encourage positive feedback. One new manager was criticised for being inappropriate when he thanked a member of his team for their excellent work in a team meeting. He was told that he should have said it privately and not caused the member of staff embarrassment.

Looking at the games played out within the particular organisation can give an insight into the culture that you are being asked to work with. Is the whole culture based on games and ulteriors so that people have no idea what is really expected of them?

Bullying games are usually played from Critical Parent to Child. The insecure manager, supervisor or boss who is coming from the position of 'you cannot trust people' plays out a classic TA game. The aim of the game is to catch people out, to make them feel so anxious that they do make mistakes. This then becomes the proof that the manager's assertion that 'you cannot trust people' is correct. This payoff can be achieved for the bully by giving insufficient information, leaving unclear instructions or lying about the instructions that he did give, setting unrealistic deadlines and putting his staff in an untenable position. The staff end up feeling bad, like children in trouble again and never being able to do anything right. This game in TA language is called NIGYSOB, 'Now I got you, son of a bitch'. It is a very destructive organisational game as it can affect the victim's performance review, his pay and his promotion prospects.

Pointing out to someone that this is happening for them and that they are allowing themselves to get hooked into the destructive behaviour can help them to re-connect with their Adult Ego State and stop playing the game.

'Courtroom' is another game in TA that can be played out within organisations. This game stems from childhood feelings of inadequate parental praise constant competition within the family. Each child wants to be seen as right to compensate for the feeling that 'I'm always wrong'. Examples of this game can be seen when an individual realises that a complaint is going to be made against them for their bullying behaviours and they 'get in quickly' and put in a counter-claim of bullying against the victim. Another example is a situation where two people have been screaming and yelling at each other across the desk and behaving inappropriately for years, when all of a sudden one of them puts in a formal complaint of bullying against the other without having mentioned anything to the other person first.

If someone feels that they are always wrong, it is much easier to project that guilt onto another person than carrying it with them, which is painful. They can feel good even if only superficially and temporarily.

'Courtroom' can be sorted out successfully with mediation, because, once aware of the game, both parties can feel heard and be 'right'. (See Chapter 15.)

Another TA game that can be played out in organisations is 'Uproar'. It begins with a gentle discussion in which two people exchange views on a particular issue. Gradually the discussion becomes more heated and the psychological tension mounts with each person believing that they are right and their colleague is wrong. Eventually, all politeness dissipates; both end up saying exactly what they think of the other person's ideas, and it can degenerate further if they begin hurling insults at each other. The situation will become even worse if they bring in outside people to join in on one or both sides.

Probably the game that is played most often, and can be seen in terms of bullying behaviours, is Karpman's drama triangle (Karpman, 1968). The Persecutor begins by bullying the Victim

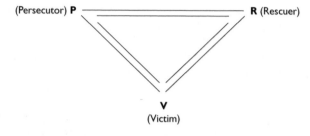

in some way. The Rescuer then asks them to stop. The switch in the game comes when the Victim turns on the Rescuer for some reason: perhaps from fear of the situation getting worse or simply because they devalue their own self-worth and believe that they deserve to be treated in the way the Persecutor was treating them. The result is the Rescuer feels persecuted by the Victim and decides not to get involved again. The Victim feels bad for having upset someone, while Persecutor (bully) is free to carry on with their unacceptable behaviours.

Games can be played over varying periods – from a few minutes to a lifetime. They have certain recognisable qualities. First, they are repetitive and have a certain 'here we go again quality', so that an observer and even the players can predict the outcome. Then, there is an ulterior transaction, i.e., an unspoken message under- neath the overt communication. There is a switch where the ulterior message is identified and addressed by the recipient. Either all the parties involved end up feeling bad or there is a win/lose element. One person feels self-righteous and the other person feels bad. The key to all of this behaviour is that it is played outside of conscious awareness. We, as part of the game, will have been part of the same scenario on many occasions. All the participants are likely to have played the same game/scenario on many occasions with the same outcome.

Berne writes that there are three degrees of games. First degree could be 'Uproar' played out as an argument in a public meeting; second degree could be 'Uproar' played out as a blazing row behind closed doors; third degree could be played out between manager and subordinate and ends with the subordinate being dismissed. This can easily happen in cases of bullying where it is a senior member of staff's word against a more junior member's and the one who is more subordinate is encouraged to resign.

Hay (1988), in her discussion of games in organisations, echoes this idea when she says the games have recognisable qualities and outcomes that range from mild to severe.

I have dealt with cases of bullying that can be compared to collecting food stamps. What happens is that a manager, for instance, 'collects' incidents of behaviour and 'hoards' them away. The manager may be irritated by a member of the team who does not perform their tasks in a required way. This can go on for some time, with the manager choosing not to say anything about it. Suddenly, and without warning, they overreact to a specific previously ignored incident and shout and scream out of all proportion to the infraction. Or, they keep all these 'stamps' saved up until appraisal time, when they give the staff member a low grade or no pay rise.

For more in-depth understanding of the usefulness of TA when working with human beings in any setting see Stewart and Joines (1987) and Hay (1988).

Gestalt

The third psychological theory that I find useful when thinking about organisations is Gestalt. Clarkson (1989) compares Gestalt to a family made up of individual members, each with their own individual psychology. Each individual member acts without reference to the others. However, the family also operates as a systemic whole, which is more than and different from the sum total of the individual psychologies of the family members. This way of looking at families can be applied to organisations. Each team within an organisation can be seen as 'separate individuals' – each with their individual psychology yet, when put together, running as a systemic whole. This analogy can be used throughout the organisation as the group gets larger and larger until it encompasses the whole organisation.

Organisational cultures are wholes (gestalts) that can only be fully appreciated by those forming part of the whole. Understanding a culture from the outside requires the ability of empathic understanding, which Hofstede (1991) considers to be a major advantage for the consultant working with management. It allows consultants to develop an approach to their work that is compatible with the particular organisation's needs. It also enables them to see more clearly where in the organisation problems lie and consequently propose changes to those areas and not others where the outcome may be unpredictable.

The number of people in an organisation equals the number of individual pathologies interrelating together. Each one of us has a different pathology, acquired in childhood and affected by life experiences along the way, making us unique individuals. This programming of who we are is not set solid; we are capable of adapting and changing. Hofstede (1991) refers to this as the 'software of the mind'.

People add their uniqueness to many cultures, they learn how to adapt and fit in while maintaining their own survival skills. They are part of a family culture and have had experience of school, youth group and often higher education cultures. Moreover, they choose to belong to other cultures: the gym, the golf club, bridge or drama group. Within the organisation they work together and form the work culture. Stapley (1996) refers to this as the personality of the organisation. The work culture develops over time and although the employees may not be totally happy with it they understand how it operates and what to expect of it. Therefore, they are frequently reluctant to see changes to it.

Similarly, certain behaviours and beliefs that have developed over time form part of the culture, and people want to keep them as they are. In one organisation, the respected manager of many years' standing always gave each member of his team half a day extra holiday in December to do their Christmas shopping. This was unofficial – his way of thanking them for all their hard work during the year – and it had become one of the rituals in that department. Problems arose when the manager retired and the new manager didn't agree with this ritual, preferring to reward the team members only if they met their targets and achieved set profit margins.

Rituals can be company wide (e.g., an annual social occasion) or peculiar to certain groups of people developing their own group habits (e.g., buying cakes for the whole team on their birthdays).

In addition, cultures develop sets of values – overt or covert – and these form part of the group norms. People in the organisation might complain about management to each other but they are fiercely loyal and defensive on hearing criticism from outside. Examples of this can be seen when a merger takes place; people who previously complained about aspects of their organisation become defensive when 'new' people come in and start making the same complaints. People who complain are often outraged at the suggestion of moving to another organisation.

Cruel banter and sarcasm can become the norm in some families and organisations, which makes it more difficult to change the culture to one of dignity and respect for all. 'Fred doesn't mind everyone being rude to him, everyone has treated him like that for years.' Sometimes they are shocked to learn that Fred does mind but has always been too afraid to say anything for fear of making an uncomfortable situation worse.

Symbols are another component of organisational culture. They usually take the form of coded signs or methods of communicating that only those people on the inside understand (e.g., jargon, nicknames, gestures, greeting, objects or dress and style codes). In one call centre, all the PCs had various symbols (toys or objects) on them, a teddy bear, a 'Telly Tubby', 'Hedwig the Owl', or the latest cult symbol. Over time, some of the symbols will have changed, as fashion changes, yet the identity as part of the culture will remain. Stapley (1996) considers it to be invaluable for the consultant to understand the symbols of the organisation and share the common language before being able to help in the process of change. By not taking the time to understand these symbols, they are putting themselves at risk of taking retrograde steps when facing defensive reactions to an 'outsider' instead of being able to move forward as 'part of' the organisation. In whatever capacity you are employed by an organisation, if people see you as batting on their team and for their benefit you are likely to attract goodwill. A team alienated from the consultant or their ideas will stop co-operating and can make the consultant's task difficult.

The Gestalt concept of boundaries is useful when dealing with a team that is anxious and scared. There may also be some unspoken paranoia, such as 'Is the consultant coming in to see how well we do our jobs and prepare the company to get rid of us?' By acknowledging and respecting the personal boundaries of the team members, they are less likely to become anxious, which in turn affects their ability to think clearly. Hirschhorn (1997) suggests that people in organisations create subjective boundaries in order to contain their anxieties. By labelling a person who is responsible for bullying (e.g., 'He is always a tyrant . . .'), people are in effect colluding with the behaviour and justifying not doing anything about it. Similarly, by putting a subjective boundary around the victim they don't need to deal with the issues. Keeping the victim separate, making them different and not part of the team, takes away any group responsibility for the way they are being treated. The consultant needs to recognise these subjective boundaries and bring them to the conscious awareness of the group.

An organisation is a whole and is dependent on each part interrelating to the others. By dealing with individuals and groups where difficulties have arisen, positive changes can take place. Menzies Lyth (1988) refers to this by stating that major organisational change cannot take place by decision-making alone (e.g., policies being written); she sees it as often involving a 'slow, gradual and often painful evolutionary process'.

Nevis (1987) refers to the phenomenon in which people become entrenched in the components of their culture and are unwilling to change as having fixed gestalts. Hanging onto their perceptions of people and past events has a disabling effect on seeing new ways positively and being able to move on to new behaviours that are more appropriate to the here and now. People do need to be heard and have the past acknowledged before they can move on. Situations like this often arise after a downsizing or rightsizing has taken place and some small groups of people are missing their colleagues, feeling guilty that they still have jobs, and generally wanting to hold onto the 'good old days' when they were all friends together.

Crichley and Casey (1989), quoted in Towler (1997), suggest that organisations, like individuals, can get 'stuck'. When consulting to an organisation, you may get the impression that an individual, or a team of individuals, is stuck. This invariably suggests that the individual or team is mirroring what is going on within the organisation.

By examining what is going on in sub-cultures within the organisation we are often able to identify just where the organisation is stuck. Working with an organisation to change areas of 'stuckness' often means introducing new policies and working with management teams to help them to accept that they had been stuck in bad policies, e.g., colluding with inappropriate behaviours from people who 'get results' at the expense of a stable workforce.

The organisational 'stuckness' may also be representative of the person at the top who is acting out childhood scenes. For example, the chief executive of an organisation gave his management team unclear instructions. When questioned, he revealed that he 'did not expect them to get it anyway' as ever since childhood he has carried a belief that he is misunderstood. After he had been taught how to communicate clearly, he stopped thinking that his management team was stupid. He also believed that he was understood and no longer stupid.

Emotional Intelligence

One of the fundamental underpinnings of Emotional Intelligence (EI) is empathic listening – something that, to seasoned counsellors and psychologists, has become second nature, at least as far as our clients are concerned. Goleman (1996) describes EI as: 'The capacity for recognising our own feelings and those of others, for motivating ourselves, and for managing emotions well, in ourselves and in our relationships.' Therefore, before we can begin to use EI in organisations, we have to start with ourselves.

Another of the fundamentals of EI is the notion that people can develop their emotional intelligence to achieve high self-awareness, manage their emotions in such a way that they are able to be 'the best that they can be'. One of the results of that process will inevitably be the ability to interact respectfully with other people.

Weisinger (1998) identifies three component parts of our emotional system: (1) the thoughts or cognitive appraisals, (2) the physiological changes or arousal actions, and (3) the behaviour or action tendencies. These three components interact with one another when we respond to an external event. Each of us responds in our own way because of our particular 'emotional context', i.e., that combination of factors that makes us uniquely who we are: our upbringing and the messages we received as children, our life experiences and our belief systems. (For example, people who have a strong sense of who they are and their role in the world are less likely to be 'thrown' by external events than people who are unsure of themselves.)

Emotional intelligence is about how to make our thoughts, feelings and behaviours work for us, taking into account our emotional context.

Thoughts/cognitive appraisals

Many of our thoughts are automatic and not especially accurate. For example, a mother who feels irritated when her son is not punctual says, 'I'll kill him; I hate it when he arrives late.' Does she actually mean 'hate' and 'kill'?

Automatic thoughts can lead directly to other automatic thoughts and, instead of looking for the truth in these thoughts, we get carried away by them. For example, 'Oh no, I have made a mistake . . . I'll get into trouble . . . I'm going to lose my job . . . my family will suffer and I will lose everything.' The reality is the person made a mistake. The emotion that they are experiencing during this time is fear.

Weisinger (1998) suggests ways of moving away from this distorted thinking, such as by not employing over-generalisations. Statements like 'I always get things wrong' are not useful and are likely to make people who use them feel more negative about themselves. Similarly, over-generalising statements about others can make us view the other person more negatively than is appropriate in the circumstances. For example, 'He never listens to me', when in fact he usually listens to you but on this occasion he was preoccupied. A good rule is to avoid using *always* and *never* as their meanings are too finite and limiting. A better word to use is sometimes. Weisinger discourages destructive labelling such as 'She's an idiot' and 'I'm so stupid' because these set up a belief that nothing can be done to put it right. Similarly, we should monitor our thought processes to get rid of the 'rules' we make for others, and ourselves (e.g., 'He should mow his lawn regularly', 'I must not eat chocolate', etc.).

By developing positive and avoiding negative inner dialogue we can avoid the constant inner berating of ourselves and others. Start by owning the feeling and then move on constructively. For example, 'I'm really upset with myself for making a mistake . . . I did it because I misheard some figures being dictated to me over the telephone and because I was in a rush I did not repeat them back to the sender . . . of course this does not mean I will lose my job, cause my family to suffer, or lose everything . . . instead I must go and tell my boss and ask what I can do to put it right.' Stop holding onto the negatives but recall the positive things you have done: 'I am usually totally accurate and get things done well within my deadlines.'

Physiological changes/arousal action

The next component on Weisinger's list is emotional arousal. When emotionally aroused, our rates of respiration, heartbeat, perspiration and blood pressure increase. While these physiological changes are a sign of arousal, they do not indicate whether the arousal is positive or negative. For example, if someone opens a letter containing news that makes them angry or one containing exciting news that delights them, the physiological measurements will be the same. By acknowledging these physiological changes we give ourselves the opportunity to deal with them and save ourselves the experience of anxiety or fear. By ignoring our arousal levels we run the risk of acting impulsively and without thought. As human beings we are programmed with a 'flight or fight' response. This was useful in our days of hunting in dangerous places; now, however, we need to think about what the best response to a situation will be. Expressions such as 'shooting from the hip', or 'putting the mouth into gear without engaging the brain' are examples of people reacting to situations at an emotional level without thinking first.

This idea is compatible with Goleman (1996), who says of emotional arousal that the more emotionally aroused someone is, the more the thinking part of the brain is 'hijacked'.

When we have become emotionally aroused at an inappropriate time or place, we should use constructive inner dialogue to calm ourselves down. For example, use your own name and tell yourself to take a few slow, deep breaths and you will find it is physiologically impossible to do this, panic, and fly into a rage at the same time. Once we have reduced our level of emotional arousal we are then in a position to stop and think about the most expedient way of dealing with the situation.

Behaviour/action tendencies

We can change our destructive behaviours only if we recognise them in the first instance. Many of our behaviour patterns in response to events are so automatic that we would have to stop and really think about what they are. Examples are bending paper clips when anxious, shouting when angry or smiling sardonically when about to deliver bad news. Looking at our behaviour patterns and how they help or hinder us in our daily lives is a starting point to making changes for the better. Being silent and freezing when someone in authority speaks to us may have been the way in which we learnt to survive an aggressive family; however, as grown-ups in a situation where a response is expected we need to act accordingly. Examining our behaviour patterns can enable us to become more emotionally aware and in control, so that our conscious behaviours work for us instead of against us.

Only by understanding emotional intelligence and how it works for ourselves, can we use it to help our clients in organisations deal with events and their responses to those events.

Goleman (1996) describes emotional intelligence as: 'The capacity for recognising our own feelings and those of others, for motivating ourselves, and for managing emotions well, in ourselves and in our relationships.'

Chapter 12

Counselling in organisations

If an organisation wants to be seen as having a 'human side', counselling can no longer be regarded as an 'optional extra'. In fact, Orlans and Edwards (2001) suggest that organisations are no longer asking *whether* they should have counselling, but what form it should take. They believe that failing to see counselling as part of their system is highly disadvantageous to organisations that acknowledge its relevance merely as an add-on in times of crisis.

More and more organisations are employing counsellors for a variety of reasons, among them reducing absenteeism due to on-the-job stress or to minimise the risk of litigation that might arise as a result of a stressful environment.

Benefits of integrating counsellors into an organisation

- They provide support for Human Resources in launching new policies.
- They can help employees to become fully functioning members of staff more quickly after a crisis either at work or in their personal life.
- On the flip side, they can help the colleagues of the person who is returning to work. Colleagues are often confused and don't know how to treat someone who has suffered a traumatic event in their lives. The counsellor can act as a liaison, asking the person how they want their colleagues to treat them.
- They can offer help to employees in managing both personal problems and those generated from working with their colleagues in the organisation.

Working as a counsellor within organisations can be both rewarding and complicated. Some organisations employ in-house counsellors on a contractual or staff contract basis.

Hay (1988) identifies three interrelated parts of the contract – administrative, professional and psychological. All three parts need to be negotiated and considered.

The *administrative* contract establishes where and when sessions will take place, and covers issues such as:

- What can the counsellor offer in terms of physical arrangements? Are these arrangements suitable and do they offer a confidential space? Is there an adequate and private waiting area for clients?
- How is the service advertised and accessed? Is there a nationwide helpline through which clients can refer themselves? Can clients access counsellors on a drop-in basis at certain times or do they always need to book appointments with a receptionist? Do clients need to be referred to counsellors by management or human resources?
- What provisions are in place to cover the counsellor's leave periods or unexpected sickness?
- Have sufficient time and financial resources been set aside to cover adequate supervision for the counsellor?
- Has the counsellor been provided with adequate office equipment and similar tools to enable them to do their job properly (e.g., computer, the correct stationery, etc.)?

The *professional* part of the contract is about (1) the process between the counsellor and the client, and (2) the level of accountability the organisation expects the counsellor to have towards them in terms of the sharing of information.

- How does the counsellor deal with the issue of confidentiality with the client? Towler (1997) suggests a 'statement of understanding', which the counsellor presents to each client at the beginning of the session. This outlines the nature of confidentiality and areas of client disclosure required to be known by the organisation (e.g., financial irregularities, abuse, drug misuse, criminal activity). Both client and counsellor should sign the document.

- The professional contract between the counsellor and the client explains what counselling is and what it is not, the number of sessions available and the level of outside help available.
- What are the arrangements with regard to reporting to management and personnel? Will the client be entitled to see a copy of any written report sent to the management?

With the *psychological* contract, the counsellor establishes with the client what they can reasonably expect from counselling and what a realistic contract between them is in the circumstances. The client may otherwise fantasise that the counsellor is 'their friend' who will be on their side. They will ultimately be disappointed if in the early stages a healthy 'psychological distance' is not established between them.

In the following section I list some elements of practical advice in the form of things that you, the counsellor, *should* do, followed by a section on pitfalls to be *avoided*.

Organisational counsellors need to:

1   Juggle the three-cornered contract (see Chapter 11) by reconciling the different elements. For example, you are employed by the organisation to work with individuals who are also employed by the same organisation. If the situation arises in which you cannot keep confidential from the organisation certain issues your client has revealed to you, you must be prepared to inform the client that this is the case.
2   Work with short-term focused contracts.
3   Have a firm understanding of boundaries and the issues of confidentiality. Know the organisation's policy with regard to confidentiality. Does it conflict with any professional standards that you need to maintain?
4   Have an understanding of the dynamics and culture of the organisation.
5   Have regular supervision, preferably with someone outside the organisation.
6   Be prepared for the fact that on some occasions you will be the dumping ground for the client's anger against the employer. As such, the client may be late for appointments or not turn up at all, believing the counsellor represents the company because the company is paying.

7   Have clearly stated contracts with the organisation as to what is expected of the counsellor.

8   Clearly define your own and establish the organisational stance on ethical issues.

9   Be prepared to make full and detailed assessments of the case. Poor assessment can result in a lot of wasted time and effort.

10   Establish clearly with the organisation what is on offer to employees after the initial assessment. Can a counsellor offer a number of further sessions on their own initiative or does there need to be a further referral by the organisation before this can take place? Is there external EAP provision to which the employee can be referred? Does the employee have private medical insurance? Can you refer back out into the voluntary sector, private sector or general practitioner, depending on the nature of the issue? Does the employee need referring to another department of the organisation, e.g. occupational health?

Pitfalls for organisational counsellors

1   Avoid getting hooked into and supporting (and thus colluding with) the organisation's dysfunction. Don't collude with a bullying culture. This can be avoided by getting to know and understand the organisation's culture before agreeing to work in it.

2   Avoid doing a manager's job for them. For example, a client may be sent to the counsellor to deal with their lateness, insubordination or perceived 'attitude problem'.

3   Educate the organisation as to how you see your role and what is realistically achievable in short-term work.

4   Establish a service that is confidential and separate from management control.

5   Ensure that your role in the organisation is well understood by the rest of the 'caring' team, i.e., Human Resources personnel, the welfare officer and the occupational staff. This will avoid role conflict and consequent difficult working relationships.

6   Pre-empt the situation of management expecting you to divulge confidential information relating to the client. Educate management and Human Resources that the relationship between you and the client(s) is confidential and that they have to respect it.

Chapter 13

Working with the various parties

A parallel can be drawn between individuals seeking psychotherapy and organisations seeking consultants. A person may have known after a traumatic event in childhood that they might benefit from some kind of professional help, but it is only when life events present them with another crisis that they decide to seek it.

Organisations are not necessarily any different. They are usually aware that the morale of the staff is low and that many highly competent people are 'voting with their feet', especially from certain departments. They know that they would benefit from looking at what is going on. Nothing, however, gets done until some event takes place, and possibly it is only from a fear of litigation that they finally decide to do something about it and call in outside help.

As a psychologist or counsellor working in organisations, you will be called upon to take on many different roles – all within the field of harassment or bullying in the workplace. One day you may be counselling a victim; another day and another organisation may see you counselling the accused; or you may be counselling people in Human Resources, advising them on policy matters and training them in a range of skills.

This chapter deals with the range of services you can provide and the skills you will use to do so.

Working with the victim/s

In extreme cases, we find ourselves dealing with a person whose self-esteem has been destroyed by another or others. The client may have a history of having been bullied as a child by their siblings, their parents or by children or teachers at school. They may display a typical victim-like behaviour – expecting the world to treat them badly and feeling that they do not deserve to be treated any better. None of this is important though, as our role is to help the client to overcome the latest episodes of bullying using the skills that we have gained over the years of working with individuals.

Often, they don't realise that they are being bullied because their histories have inured them to this kind of behaviour. As I hear their stories and am able to show them what is really happening, their responses are usually a mixture of shock, relief and frequently tears.

Many of these individuals do not even know whether their company has a policy that can protect them. The policy, if well written, will actually state the procedures. Our task here is to help the client to understand what these procedures are likely to entail in practice.

In the first instance, when people decide to do something about their situation they are empowered and believe themselves to be more in control. In some cases, not much more is needed than for the victim to approach the bully and explain how they are being affected. Of course, this may not work in other cases. In any event, it is not advisable to suggest that someone who is being bullied should approach the perpetrator alone; they should always take a colleague (preferably one who has witnessed the behaviour) along with them. In severe situations, it will be clear to the counsellor that the only recourse open to the victim is to seek a remedy under the policies and rules.

An important point to bear in mind is that people can be affected by bullying even if they are not the direct victims. Some people who have witnessed bullying at work – even if it happened years ago – can be suffering from 'survivor guilt'. They still feel that there must have been something that they could have done and feel guilty. I treated someone who said, 'I watched [her] destroy that man's career and I was too scared of her to say or do anything. I wasn't even friendly to him, as I didn't want to be the next in line.'

Practical steps in counselling victims

1 Working with a victim of harassment or bullying can happen at any stage in the process. Whatever the stage, the counsellor/

psychologist needs to listen to the story and normalise the feelings of the victim.

2   During the early stages their colleagues, family, Human Resources or they themselves have decided they need help. The individual knows that they feel bad and that this is a direct consequence of someone else's behaviour towards them. In cases at this early stage they need encouraging to tell their story and keep notes of times, places, details of events and who may have witnessed any of the incidents. At this stage it may be the role of the counsellor/psychologist to identify that they are being harassed or bullied and compare the behaviours to the company policy.

3   People may be afraid of doing anything about the way in which they are being treated, for different reasons, such as a fear of retaliation or just afraid of 'getting someone into trouble'. Listen to the person and ask then what they have already done about the behaviour of others and what they would be prepared to do. It may be enough for them to ask the person to 'stop'. Encourage them to take a colleague with them for support when they do this as it could make the situation worse if they go alone and they will be even more vulnerable. Fortunately, in some cases the behaviour does stop and is accompanied by an apology.

4   In other more extreme cases the incidents may be so gross that the individual is traumatised and a post-trauma debriefing is necessary before the client can think about the way forward for them.

5   In other cases, some of the bullying behaviours towards them may have triggered events from the past. They may have been bullied at school, had a bullying parent, or be an ex or current battered partner. Being humiliated in some way about their intellect may result in them feeling like a six-year-old who was shouted at for getting their sums wrong.

6   Working with someone with a history of being bullied requires care and time to help them rebuild their self-esteem as the grown-up person they are now. Help them to let go of the past, acknowledge that they deserve to be treated well and recognise when they are not.

7   For some people who have been bullied in various ways all their lives, their experience of you may be their first experience of really being listened to and heard.

Working with the accused

Working with someone accused of harassment and bullying can be as varied as working with the victims.

A counsellor/psychologist can be called in to work with the accused at any stage in the process.

Early in the process

The accused may have been referred through their Human Resources departments or by way of a self-referral through their EAP provider. You may be called in during the early stages after the official written complaint has been made.

Some people are likely to present with genuine shock; someone who they considered to be their friend is now bringing a complaint against them. They may even be saying that they are the one who is being bullied and they should be bringing the complaint.

Whatever the circumstances, feelings are likely to be intense whether arising out of hurt or anger.

Steps to be followed

1   Listen to their story.
2   Ask to see the written complaint – work with facts and not the highly emotional individual's interpretation of what is being said.
3   Explain to them how their company policy works and what is likely to happen next.
4   Discourage them from gossiping to other people and trying to get allies on their side.
5   Explore the possibility of asking a colleague to attend the interviews with them to offer support.
6   Help them think through whether there are any witnesses they can call who would be willing to go forward and state their case.
7   Offer genuine support – even if their style is that of a self-righteous bully, they are still human beings and deserve to be respected as such and treated well.
8   If relevant, do point out how you are experiencing the way in which they are treating you. For example: 'I feel patronised by you when you say that, and I am wondering if that is your

intention.' (This is useful feedback for them, especially if their behaviour is outside of conscious awareness; explain that they would not be presenting themselves in a favourable light with the investigator from the outset.)

From experience, I have found that most people in this situation will want you to like them and be on their side. If the complaints are not substantiated they may or may not change their behaviour.

When the accused is found guilty

The more challenging work for a counsellor/psychologist is working with people who have contravened the company policy on harassment and bullying.

In some instances, as part of an investigator's recommendations, an individual is encouraged to undergo counselling/professional development. These people may attend because they believe that you can help them put things at work right, help them find manipulative ways of not getting caught again, or help them to save their jobs.

Steps to be followed

1   Insist on seeing all the paperwork on:
    (a) accusations,
    (b) findings.
    This enables you to work with full facts and not the subjective version from the client.
2   Enable client to understand the impact on others of their behaviour and why they have ended up in the situation they have.
3   Some history exploring may be relevant as the client finds it difficult to understand the difference between acceptable and unacceptable behaviour in the workplace. They may be modelling behaviour in the workplace that they learnt as young apprentices from their line managers, or even earlier from teachers or family members. One woman was shocked to learn that the conduct of her much revered, now deceased, father on whose style of management she had based her own, would not be acceptable today.

4   Do model a respectful way of working with the person no matter how serious the findings.

5   The role of the counsellor/psychologist in these circumstances is that of an educator, teaching people new ways of behaving in the workplace that will be acceptable. Depending on the client, explaining emotional literacy or TA games may help this process (see Chapter 11).

6   Probably the most important aspect in working with someone found guilty of contravening the company policy is their accepting responsibility for their behaviour. Wanting to blame others, the organisation and the system are all common reactions. In some senses, all may be valid arguments and in order to make significant behaviour changes the individual has to be prepared to accept their part in it, and take adult responsibility for the effect their behaviour has on others. It is not just the victim/s, but also the witnesses, managers, Human Resources staff and anyone else involved in the case that may be affected. For instance, their own families may have become involved and stressed as a consequence.

If the individual is unwilling to take responsibility, they are unlikely to change their behaviour at any real level. It quickly becomes apparent when one is working with people who are just paying lip service to behaviour changes.

On the other hand, working with people who accept that their behaviour at work is unacceptable can be rewarding. With an eagerness to change they are happy to accept feedback, even though some is not as palatable as they would like.

Be willing to give honest feedback in a constructive, non-persecutory way. Negative feedback is helpful only if alternative suggestions are given alongside it. Part of professional development is teaching someone to do it differently. One woman was so delighted with the fundamental changes that she made at work as they had a knock-on effect in her private life. On one occasion when her dry cleaner had made a mistake, instead of ranting she worked with them to put it right and felt good about herself as a consequence.

Working with the witnesses

Witnesses may be first hand – i.e., they actually saw what happened and did nothing to defend their colleague. People who adopt this role of bystander out of fear of being the next victim often feel guilty.

1   Allow the witness to tell their story and express how they felt about what happened.
2   Explain to them that feeling guilty is 'normal' when we believe we have let someone else down. It may be that they want to talk to their victimised colleague and apologise for letting them down.
3   Explaining to them how the company policy works and what their role would be if they were willing to come forward as a witness may help to allay any fears about the formal process should it get that far.

Other witnesses may be second hand; these are people who learn about the incidents after they have happened. Such a witness may be a manager who has had some idea of difficulties in their department and chose to ignore it hoping that things would settle down again. Now, with the situation having got out of hand, they may be chastising themselves for not dealing with the situation earlier.

1   This person may be needing professional development and management skills to enable them to put things right as far as possible.
2   Managers may need support and be taught some strategies for dealing with their team members: the accused, the victim and the witnesses.
3   Alternatively, managers may need support in carrying out the tasks as part of the internal investigation team.
4   Once the investigations are over, and as part of normalising the team, the manager may need some help in devising ways of team building.
5   As part of their own professional development the manager may want to explore ways of using their learning from this tasking experience not to repeat the process again. This can be achieved by explaining the following techniques and management skills:
    (a) listening to their staff,
    (b) creating a culture of honesty,
    (c) modelling acceptable behaviours even in social situations,

    (d) treating all staff with dignity and respect,

    (e) being an advocate of, and demonstrating the importance of, the company policies,

    (f) not ignoring any inappropriate behaviours by any member of staff to another.

Working with Human Resources personnel

Many Human Resources personnel feel out of their depth when dealing with issues of harassment and bullying. They know the procedures as they are laid out in the organisation's Dignity at Work policy. What many – especially junior and inexperienced – staff members are not aware of is the level of emotion they are going to be subjected to and dealing with. As the professional outsider you can assist them in the following ways:

1   Listen to their story and the effect it is having on them.
2   You may be required to act as supervisor (many Human Resources personnel, even if counselling is part of their role, do not have official and professional supervision). They may want to talk to you about what they have done so far to confirm that they are 'getting it right'.
3   Human Resources personnel may be expected to deal with allegations of harassment and bullying against people in the organisation who are more senior than they are. They may be expected to approach these people, of whom they may be afraid themselves, to confront them with the allegations against them. What they could be wanting from you is professional help in dealing with these situations.
4   Human Resources personnel are not exempt from their own pathology. They may be reminded of a time in their lives when they were harassed or bullied. They may have found it difficult to talk to either of the parties involved due to fear. One of the parties may have reminded them of someone outside the organisation they were scared of either in the past or currently. For example, the victim may remind them of their mum or another member of their family, and consequently they find themselves unable to listen to the accused fairly and without pre-judging them as being in the wrong before an investigation is carried out.

5   Human Resources personnel may simply need the objective support of the counsellor/psychologist to enable them to carry out their jobs fairly and with as little emotional cost to themselves as possible.

Working as a trainer

Working as a trainer, especially in residential settings, often provides the opportunity to see a sub-system of the organisation at work. Issues frequently emerge which can be dealt with either as part of the training or, if this is not appropriate, the individual concerned should be referred on for counselling or professional development.

Training in the field of harassment and bullying takes many forms:

- *Awareness training* often combining the launch of a new or revised policy.
- *Management skills and professional development* for dealing with harassment and bullying.
- *Training internal personnel in harassment investigation.*
- *Training internal personnel as harassment counsellors/buddies or advisers* to give first-line advice and act as the first option for the person being harassed or bullied.

Before accepting the contract, find out:

1   as much as possible about the organisational culture – this enables the trainer to use relevant examples in their role plays, etc.;
2   whether the company has a separate Dignity at Work policy or if harassment and bullying is covered as part of its equal opportunities policy; ask for a copy so you can refer to it during the training;
3   by asking the following direct questions, about the client group:
   (a) who will attend?
   (b) are the attendees mixed in terms of status?
   (c) is the course compulsory? If not, how are the delegates selected?

(d) is a senior member of staff intending to come in and
    introduce the course or are they planning to stay for the
    course? Be clear at this stage that only participants may
    stay and that senior people popping in and out is destruc-
    tive and changes the dynamics of the group. If they do not
    intend to stay, arrangements can be made for them to come
    in at the end of the course and collect relevant feedback;
4   what the organisation requires in terms of feedback;
5   what routes are open for the client group to feed back to
    management;
6   whether the company has an EAP provider that the trainer can
    refer an individual to if the need arises;
7   if the organisation has expectations in terms of the way in
    which material is presented;
8   whether the organisation wants you to present your material or
    write their own;
9   if the organisation is unionised and what their stand on the
    course is.

Training in harassment and bullying awareness

1   Establish the level of awareness of the company policy.
2   Work with the group to define harassment and bullying.
3   Invite people to think about their own experiences of harass-
    ment and bullying. Encourage people to work in pairs or small
    groups and talk to each other about their own experiences.
4   Introduce the company policy and invite ideas about how the
    seriousness of the document could be communicated to the rest
    of the staff.
5   Work with the group to establish what they consider their role
    is in working towards an organisation with dignity and respect
    as the ethos.

Training in management skills and professional development

First steps:

1   Contract with the group for confidentiality. Explain that it is
    acceptable to go back to the office or home and talk about
    their own experience but not about that of their colleagues.

2   Contract with them as to what they would hope to get out of the course and what they may have to give up in order to achieve this.

3   Emphasise that the importance of good modelling and good management is creating a healthy productive workforce where dignity and respect for everyone is the norm.

4   Establish how individuals see themselves as a manager and what sort of feedback they have had from their staff. (Sometimes this can have been done formally in advance so that people come to the training having asked for and received 360-degree feedback from both senior and junior colleagues.) Have they had any surprises from their feedback?

5   Invite people to think about what behaviours in themselves they would like to change and contract with the group towards making the first steps aimed at achieving this.

By teaching managers *emotional intelligence* skills as part of their own professional development, they can develop them and become equipped to model the skills for their staff. Practical emotional development skills can be divided into various stages:

Stage I: Self-awareness

The more self-aware a person is, the greater their accuracy in predicting how they will behave in a given situation. If a person finds themselves in a position in which they have to interact with someone else with whom they have a history of not getting along, the self-aware person can make allowances for this and prepare themselves to do things differently this time.

If a manager/supervisor is aware of what irritates them, they can look at the validity of this behaviour and its effect on others. They can ask themselves whether they are projecting someone from a non-work environment or someone from their past onto a work colleague. This can happen outside of conscious awareness for many reasons. For example, the receptionist's voice may have the same intonation – or she may use the same language structure – as a much-feared schoolteacher, with the result that a manager is afraid to approach her about her inappropriate and bullying behaviour towards others.

Once the individual is aware of this they can begin to handle the receptionist as the man or woman they are and not confer upon them the undeserved attributes of the teacher. In this way they will become enabled to deal with what is relevant in the here and now.

Self-awareness is about an individual's looking at themselves in all the roles they carry out. Asking themselves questions about, e.g., what their praise/negative feedback pattern is. Do they give only criticism? Is their attitude to giving praise 'If you were doing something wrong I would have told you'?

Or, do they ask themselves if they are sufficiently self-aware to be able to own any bullying or harassing behaviours they themselves may be guilty of, currently or in the past? Do they collude with bullying and harassment in their department by either joining in or turning a blind eye?

Do they think about what the effect of their behaviours may have been on the recipients?

Self-awareness is therefore about being aware of and owning our own feelings. It is not wrong to feel angry about something that has happened; it is wrong, however, to act out those feelings on others.

Teach delegates to identify their own emotions and corresponding behaviours. For example, do you shout at people and get angry when you are feeling vulnerable and your own manager has criticised your performance? Do you get angry when your subordinates expect you not only to carry out your own role but manage them as well?

Criticisms that make us angriest are those which contain a grain of truth. If someone accuses us of something that is totally absurd and out of the question, we can shrug it off because it feels not relevant to us. If we are accused of something that we either have or have not done and we feel guilty about it, this kind of criticism is more likely to get us angry.

A practical example of this is seen where a member of the team hands in their notice and the manager takes it personally and acts in a bullying manner towards them throughout their notice period.

The concept of emotional literacy is useful here: teaching people how to express their feelings. For example, being able to honestly express the following: 'When you arrive late after every break on my course it makes me feel upset and undervalued by you and I believe that you don't respect me as a person.'

In summary, becoming self-aware is not about becoming self-critical or self-berating and taking every opportunity to remind others of our faults. Being self-aware is to acknowledge that we have made, and will make, mistakes because we are human, having the humility to own them and doing what we can to put them right.

Stage II: Listening skills

Another key to emotional intelligence is listening. Many people believe they are listening when in fact they are pretending to look interested while simply biding their time and waiting for their turn to speak.

Teaching basic listening skills to managers can prove to be invaluable. Working in an experiential group they not only have an opportunity to learn how to really listen to others but also to gain the experience of being really heard by another person.

Stage III: Communicating to be heard

In order for others to understand the message we are communicating we need to know what we want to say. Unfortunately, there is frequently confusion about what an individual thinks they have said to others and what those others actually hear.

Rules of communication:

1 Be clear – to avoid misunderstanding.
2 Be concise.
3 Be honest.
4 Own your own feelings – use 'I' statements and not 'one', 'they' or 'we'.

Giving feedback:

1 Be relevant.
2 Talk about the person's behaviour and not them as a person.
3 Give them alternative ways of dealing with the situation.
4 Be concise – avoid waffling and creating confusion.
5 Be prepared to deal with the other person's feelings.
6 Consider how you would feel if given this message in this particular way.
7 Give positive and negative feedback with the same care – some people find it difficult to hear anything positive about themselves.
8 Remember that feedback needs to be a two-way process.

Receiving feedback:

1   Listen carefully to the full statements and avoid cutting the person off before they have finished.
2   Only accept what is relevant to you; for instance, if you are told that you are late and stupid and, in fact, you were late, acknowledge that. Apologise for being late but say that being late does not make you stupid and you therefore will not accept that part of the criticism.
3   Be prepared to think through ways of doing things differently.
4   Accept sometimes that being given unpalatable feedback can be positive as it provides an opportunity for change and to do something about your behaviour – especially if others have alluded to similar dissatisfaction with your behaviour in the past.

ASSERTIVENESS SKILLS

Teaching managers to be assertive without being aggressive can help them put into practice and to model the clear communication skills that they have learnt.

By treating everyone in their department well and with respect they are not only putting into practice the company's Dignity at Work policy but also sending a clear message that the policy is taken seriously.

Stage IV: Self-care

By teaching managers to recognise symptoms of stress in themselves they are more likely to recognise when all is not well with individual members of their team.

Start by inviting managers to think about how they recognise their own stress and what their current management strategies are.

Use the group to help each other with brainstorming techniques to work out realistic ways of:

1   removing some of the major stressors from their lives – sometimes this is about dealing with situations they may have ignored in the hope that they would spontaneously go away,
2   balancing their lives so that everything is not always about dealing with a stressful working life and preparing for it.

Invite people to think about their support systems, colleagues, friends or family. Ask whether they use the support that is available to them or hold onto the belief that others wouldn't understand what they are going through.

Explain that their support system does not necessarily have to understand, and that they can get different things from different people. A friend who has no idea of what it may be like to be responsible for a team of people among whom covert bullying is occurring may be the perfect person for them to have a game of squash with and help get some balance back into their life.

Chapter 14

The process of investigation

Please refer also to Chapter 7 of this manual where the theory of harassment investigations is covered in greater detail.

Preparation

Take a thorough brief from the organisation before beginning any work.

Agree on a time-based fee rather than on the theoretical 'price' of work. Investigations can grow as more witnesses for both sides are brought forward, so you need to allow for this.

Establish practicalities

1   When will you be carrying out the interviews?
2   Where will you be carrying out the interviews? (Remember that off-site is often the most appropriate. If you can, try to suggest this alternative.)
3   Are there toilet and tea/coffee facilities?
4   Will you be working alone and taking your own notes or do you work with a colleague?
5   Is the organisation planning to provide you with a scribe?
6   Are you recording the interviews?
7   What is the company policy in terms of having a union representative or member of staff from the organisation sitting in on the interviews?

Before the interviews

Ensure that:

1   you have read and understood any relevant paperwork and listened to any recorded voice mails before beginning the interview;

2   you have read, and have an understanding of, the company's equal opportunities policy;

3   you have established a contract with the organisation as to deadlines, the type of report they require and whether you will be expected to present it to the board;

4   there is clarity as to the kind of recommendations the organisation is expecting from you.

The interviews

All parties should be interviewed independently so that you can form an objective view of the events leading up to the complaint.

1   Ensure that the interview environment is suitable – i.e., a place where you won't be disturbed or overheard.

2   Introduce yourself to all parties as an impartial investigator; introduce any other members of the organisation who may be present.

3   Establish the purpose of the interview. Refer back to the company's Dignity at Work policy and stress their commitment to it.

4   Explain that the investigator's role is to establish, after a thorough investigation, whether there is reasonable belief that an incident or incidents took place.

5   Inform the complainant, witness or alleged perpetrator that you will be recording the interview or taking and keeping detailed notes.

6   Remind each witness of their duty to keep both the content and the facts of the interview confidential. This will maximise constructive resolution and not contribute to inevitable rumours. Reconfirm that confidentiality will be maintained by the organisation.

7   Establish the facts leading up to the event and what actually happened. When interviewing the witnesses, be sensitive and empathic in order to find out as much information as you can about the incident(s).

8   Keep detailed notes of the interview.

9 Do not be tempted to have off-the-record discussions with any of the parties. Maintain your impartiality at all times.
10 Do ask the following questions to establish the facts:
- What happened?
- Where did it happen?
- When did it happen?
- Were there any witnesses?
- Who else was involved?
- Has it happened before?
- What was the impact on you?
- Were other people affected?
- What has happened so far, e.g., 'Have you seen the harassment counsellor yet?'

In the course of the interviews, you will typically be asked what may be tricky or difficult questions. The following are some of the most common of these, with the appropriate responses:

Question	Response
Do I have to talk to you?	Respond with something like 'Why not?'
What will happen to me?	Explain the company policy on victimisation.
Do you believe me?	Both the complainant and the alleged perpetrator may ask this question. It is not your place to confirm or deny. Instead, say something like: 'It is not my role to comment; my role is to establish the facts and listen impartially to all sides.'
What will happen to him/her?	An appropriate response may be to say: 'At this stage I have no idea. A formal complaint has been raised and my role is to investigate. And that is where my role ends. I have nothing to do with any outcome, which is solely in the hands of the board of managers.'
I want them sacked.	Say something like: 'The outcome is purely dependent upon the result of the disciplinary hearing.'
You can't prove anything can you?	'It is my role to interview everyone concerned and make my decision by weighing up the evidence on the balance of probabilities.'

Points to note

- Avoid reactions that express your shock (e.g., 'That's awful, how terrible', etc.).
- Avoid counselling.
- Do take detailed notes.
- Do remain impartial.
- Manage your own embarrassment and consequently theirs.
- Summarise the response to each question.

Weighing up the evidence

Working within your brief and the company's Equal Opportunities/Dignity at Work policy, weigh the evidence using both the complainant's original allegation, interview notes and any witness statements against the accused's interview notes and any evidence they have presented.

You need to establish:

- The impact of the behaviour.
- The behaviour of all parties following the alleged incident(s).
- The consistency of the information gained from all parties.
- Any unspent past complaints (e.g., had they spoken to Human Resources in the past about the same behaviours?).
- Any witness statements that corroborate or dispute that the incident(s) took place.
- Any admissions which may have been made.

Your report must give clear details of evidence you have regarding whether the events took place. Admissions are not necessary; all that is required is a reasonable belief that an incident took place. The standard of proof required here is whether or not, on the balance of probabilities (i.e., more probable than not) an incident occurred. It is not necessary to prove that an event happened beyond reasonable doubt, which is required in police and criminal cases.

The report

Remember that what the organisation is looking to you for is your help in reaching a constructive resolution. The outcome of your investigation may result in disciplinary action being taken and, in some cases, dismissal. Consequently, what the organisation needs from the investigator is a professional and neutral report, which enables them to deal with a sensitive and stressful interpersonal area.

1   Begin by summarising the allegations you were asked to address. Indicate clearly whom you interviewed and their role within the organisation.

2   Address each allegation separately. In this way, any allegation that was not founded can be dismissed. For example: 'I found no evidence from any of the people interviewed to substantiate Allegation 4.'

3   There is a need to establish a reasonable belief that the incidents took place, after a thorough investigation which is fair to all. Follow this by giving evidence for the following:

   (a) The effect of the behaviour – e.g., person X has suffered ill health as a result of the behaviour of the accused towards them.

   (b) There are consistent, distinct and different complaints against the person.

   (c) Others corroborate the complaints.

   (d) The accused had changed their behaviour as a result of being approached by Human Resources after informal complaints regarding their management style.

   (e) It was found that on several occasions the staff had broached the difficulties with the accused and had been ignored.

   (f) Several members of staff provided a dossier of evidence.

   (g) The accused failed to acknowledge any responsibility or even any interest in the accusations. (For instance, if the response of the accused was 'Let's just forget it and move on', this would suggest that they are not understanding the gravity of the problem or the impact of their behaviour on others.) This should be clearly expressed in the report.

4   Write clear conclusions referring back to the company policy, for example:
   'The behaviour of Mrs X towards Mrs Y when she yelled and swore at her contravened section 1.2 of the company's Equal Opportunities Policy.
   'Consequently, I conclude that . . .'

Recommendations

As counsellors, we are not in a position to make recommendations as to disciplinary procedures, outcomes, etc. Nor is it appropriate for us to make suggestions, as we have only a sample of evidence about a specific case and no insight into the full history.

However, the kinds of recommendations that *it is* appropriate for the professional investigator to make are:

1   The awareness that constructive resolution could be achieved through skilled intervention (e.g., mediation).
2   Professional development for either or both parties.
3   Management skills training.
4   A mentor system to enable personal coaching to take place.

You may have agreed at the contracting stage to present your report to the board. Be prepared to stick to what your report says and not feel obliged to elaborate and put in your own opinions.

What happens next?

In some cases, an individual accused of harassment and/or bullying may own up to the behaviour and say that they did not mean to cause pain, suffering or other effects. Management may decide that an informal warning is sufficient. They may well offer the accused mentoring, coaching or decide that mediation is the way forward.

In other cases, after the report is presented the management may take into consideration other similar behaviours that have taken place in the past.

Where the board of managers considers it necessary, they may decide to implement the company's disciplinary procedures.

Taking care of yourself

Harassment investigations can be draining so be aware of the value of taking time out to allow yourself to let go. Once your report is complete and either handed in or presented *let it* go – after that point it no longer has anything to do with you. You have no right to know what happened to the alleged perpetrator – whatever your belief about their guilt. (See also Chapter 17.)

Chapter 15

Mediation

Please refer also to Chapter 8 of this manual, where the theory and processes of mediation are discussed in depth. This chapter summarises the additional considerations to be kept in mind by counsellors/ psychologists wanting to enter the field.

Mediation requires specific skills and training and there are a number of courses available. However, counsellors and psychotherapists with both the training and experience in listening already have the basic skills required for working as a mediator inside organisations.

Working as a mediator has many similarities to working as a psychotherapist with couples, with each side having their own entrenched position and views and unable to see a way out of it. My psychotherapeutic skills enable me to actively listen to both parties in an objective manner. This models good listening practices, which are necessary since a major contributing factor to disputes is that neither side is listening to the other, nor do they feel that they are being listened to.

When considering the transferable skills from being a psychotherapist to working as a mediator within organisations, Rogers's (1961) core conditions of congruence, unconditional positive regard and empathy can be taken as a basis. These help to ensure treating each side with respect and actively listening to what they have to say. TA (Berne, 1961) teaches us to recognise games and rackets which cut across and offer alternative ways of communicating by modelling and reframing (Schiff *et al.*, 1975) and emotional literacy (Steiner, 1984).

Working as a mediator within organisations would involve the counsellor/psychotherapist undergoing a short formal training.

However, they already have many of the basic skills necessary for working as a mediator.

Mediators need to be acutely aware of what they hear, see, feel and sense. This is another reason that therapists and counsellors, who are trained in being aware of covert messages, are ideally suited to working as mediators.

Switching roles – for instance, working as a counsellor in one organisation and a mediator in another – offers variety and a chance to expand many of the skills that trained counsellors and psychotherapists take for granted.

Leviton and Greenstone (1997) see the mediator who works as a facilitator providing the process by which issues in dispute can be examined jointly, common objectives found and insight gained into opposing perspectives.

The role of the mediator is to provide process facilitation. They act as chairperson to opposing factions, and maintain a climate conducive to problem-solving. They facilitate by keeping the discussion on track, intervening where appropriate to maintain communication between both parties.

The role of clarifier is often essential. A mediator should establish that both parties know what the other is talking about, sometimes asking one or other party to explain what they mean by a particular term.

It is not a mediator's role to create a solution. However, by drawing each party into hypothetical discussions they can encourage the parties to think and communicate with each other. For example, 'Have you thought about Y as a possibility?'

Another role that Leviton and Greenstone (1997) suggest the mediator may play is that of face-saver. Sometimes, by exploring a hidden agenda, a reason for non-agreement to settle may be found. For example, saying 'Tell me, what do you need in order to settle this dispute?' can be the key. Sometimes it may be as simple as receiving a written apology that their friends, family or colleagues have insisted they get and without which they would feel they had failed.

The mediator may also be required to act as an agent of reality, i.e., to point out the level of practicality that either party would consider constituted a good outcome.

Any counsellor or psychotherapist who has worked with couples or families will recognise some of the essential skills required by a mediator:

- Remain objective and impartial throughout.
- Be prepared to ask probing questions to obtain information.
- Respond to, and attempt to defuse, any mounting tensions.
- Be aware of the covert process, noticing body language, non-verbal communications and, often, what has been left out rather than what has been said.
- Establish yourself as a professional who can be trusted by building rapport and giving the disputants confidence in you. Be a calming influence on what may be a highly emotional and stressful environment.
- Be prepared to say who you are and what the purpose of mediation is, as well as its limitations. Clarify for people who may confuse it with the process of arbitration.

Many mediators find their role satisfying because they are working to achieve a win/win outcome.

Greenstone *et al.* (1991) (quoted in Leviton and Greenstone, 1997) state that 'If the parties believe that the mediator is capable of helping them reach a solution to their dispute, they will be more likely to trust the mediator and the process.'

At the end of a successful mediation, both parties sign a document stating what they are prepared to do now, and in the future, to resolve the original dispute. Although not legally binding, this document can form a potent reminder of each party's expressed desire to be as good as their word.

Finally, pitfalls to avoid when working as a mediator:

- It is not the mediator's role to solve the conflict for the parties.
- Even though you have the skills and may be tempted to intervene, you are not the psychotherapist for either party.
- Either party may try and seduce the mediator onto their side.
- Either party may want retribution.

Chapter 16

Other roles for counsellors/ psychologists

There are many roles that trained counsellors and psychologists can take within organisations. We have discussed counsellors, harassment investigators and mediators. However, there are other ways in which our skills and training can be put to good use in organisational work; these include the areas of coaching, mentoring and professional development.

Coaching

Coaching is often referred to as management coaching or executive coaching. The skills of counsellors and psychologists transfer easily to this work.

Executive coaching, the most commonly used coaching in organisations is a one-to-one relationship in which executives are prepared, trained and empowered to do the roles they are already, in many cases, undertaking. People managing from the top who have no management or people skills model inappropriate and, in some cases, bullying behaviours to the more junior staff.

Another type of coaching, management coaching, offers managers an opportunity to explore any fears and difficulties they may be experiencing in dealing with members of their team. By sharing these difficulties with a one-to-one coach the manager can be helped to find different ways of dealing with their team – with a positive outcome for all concerned.

Coaching is not psychotherapy, although many people in organisations equate listening to someone else's problems with counselling. Rather, coaching is about a process through which someone from outside the organisation, using psychological skills to equip their 'client' with the required skills, knowledge and tools, helps that person realise more of their potential within the organisation.

Sometimes a coach has to begin at a very basic level, teaching basic management, leadership and communication skills. Many people find themselves in positions of managing others without the training or preparation they ought to have had. Often, they have been promoted to the position because of their qualifications, technical ability or through a senior person's leaving, management considering it cheaper to fill the position with a more junior person who can 'do the job' but not necessarily with the people skills or even inclination to manage. These people can flounder and sometimes need to work on their basic confidence and self-esteem before any more-complicated skills can be taught.

Not only can a trained counsellor or psychologist identify when someone is stuck behind their own crippling lack of confidence and self-esteem, but s/he can also give feedback in a non-persecutory way and build an atmosphere of trust and safety in which the client can explore these issues.

If a client has been damaged by something that happened either in the current or a previous organisation, they may still be carrying the effects with them. Being given the space and support to let go of the past, they can move into the present and plan their future. They can learn to behave in ways that command respect from others and, in return, be treated with respect.

Another advantage to the organisation of using counsellor/ psychologists is that they already like, and feel comfortable with, working with people. They have a proven commitment to helping people to grow and make changes in their lives. Being a coach is about helping people to grow and make professional changes in their work. These changes have a knock-on effect in that they contribute to changes in the organisational culture by which respect becomes the norm and people are treated with dignity.

Peltier (2001) puts forward a positive case for therapists (counsellors and psychologists) adding value to the business world as coaches. They can model appropriate adult behaviour, they can listen effectively and they pose no threat or competition to the executives themselves. This latter point can be an issue with internal mentoring or buddy systems that some organisations adopt. Therapists are comfortable giving feedback (even if it is unpalatable) in a positive way to enable the client to learn from it. Trained counsellors/psychologists are unlikely to think there is something wrong with them when a client doesn't do what they agree to do. They have dealt with resistance as part of their work many times, they have come to expect it and they have ways of working through it to the client's benefit.

Practitioners used to goal-setting and contract-making in a clinical practice will find the transition to working as an executive or management coach logical. If issues do arise that are therapeutic and outside the specifications of organisational coaching, the coach will recognise them and refer the client to another counsellor/psychologist.

Landsberg (1997) compares coaching to Socrates who saw himself as the 'midwife to understanding', believing that one could help people to understand but not make them understand, just as the midwife delivers but does not give birth to the child. If one sees the coach as a 'midwife to skill building', the dilemma is whether to issue an instruction or to ask a question, or whether to use a style of interaction somewhere between these two extremes. For the psychologist/counsellor this is what they are trained to do: help people to help themselves.

Mentoring

A mentor is part of a support system within an organisation. A mentor can act as a coach to people in the organisation or, if appropriate, refer them to a specialist coach. These two roles can be, and often are, intertwined.

Clutterbuck (2002a) sees the mentor's role as invaluable in several ways to the overworked and stressed executive.

In the role of executive coach, a mentor can shadow the executive to get an insight into their world and their team. With keen observation and communication skills, mentors can offer an objective opinion on specific behavioural changes the executive should make. They can also point out the gaps in executives' skill patterns.

In the role of reflective mentor, the mentor takes a holistic approach to the executive's life and helps them to gain self-awareness. Exploring with them their repetitive patterns of getting involved in difficult work situations, mentors can then objectively, through constructive feedback, challenge and help them to do things differently in the future. They can also help the executive to design personal learning objectives and plan realistic ways of being able to adhere to these.

Both of these types of mentoring can be successfully carried out by practitioners trained in the fields of counselling and psychology.

Clutterbuck suggests that counsellors have difficulties in allowing themselves to use the skills necessary to work in executive mentoring. However, mentoring can take many forms and requires the skills readily accessible to trained counsellors and psychologists who are willing to transfer their theoretical knowledge, their knowledge of organisations and their ability to listen and understand people. To make this transfer, the major component is a shift in mindset that follows the acknowledgement and understanding that executive mentoring is not counselling and that it is possible to transfer the skills already available to take on these different organisational roles.

Coaching and mentoring in an organisational setting is as rewarding as watching people change and grow in a clinical setting; the issues and process are different but the results are the same.

Professional development

Professional development on a one-to-one basis is often recommended for people accused of bullying. It does more than simply offer a guilty party the opportunity to save their job; it also affords the individual an opportunity to identify, own and change their behaviours that have caused offence and harm.

The skills of a psychotherapist/counsellor/psychologist are ideally suited to the task of helping such individuals to recognise their own shadow side. Samuels *et al.* (1986) call this first stage the shadow confrontation. The next step consists of coming to terms with the integration of shadow material. The consultant, by creating a safe and supportive environment, both allows and encourages the client to make changes that affect not only themselves as an individual but consequently the organisation as well.

This is a different way of working for many counsellors and psychologists, and can be rewarding work if they are willing to change their attitude towards third-party involvement and move away from the traditional model of client–counsellor confidentiality. For example, if you accept a contract to work with an individual, and part of that contract is a feedback loop in the form of a report to the organisation,

- make this clear to the individual before you begin working with them, and
- agree that you will allow the client to read the report before it is delivered to the organisation.

In this way, there will be no surprises for the client and no surprises for you if the client should complain that they thought they were speaking to you in confidence.

Many different terms are used – coaching, professional development, life coaching, mentoring. Although some of the techniques and time scales may differ, the reality is that they all have a common theme of encouraging people to be the best that they can be and fulfil their own potential.

Chapter 17

Taking care of the self

Working in the field of bullying and harassment can be stressful, even for the most experienced counsellor/psychologist.

We routinely acknowledge for our clients that whatever they are feeling is normal. When they tell us that they feel they shouldn't be upset because, after all, they haven't been physically harmed by the event, we normalise this and tell them that whatever they are feeling is right for them.

Yet how often do we turn this back on ourselves? We ought to. We may have had strong reactions and feelings on hearing the details of what our bullied or harassed client experienced. We may be full of disbelief because we do not want to accept that one human being or group of human beings could behave so badly to others.

Allow yourself to have these feelings and acknowledge internally to yourself that you will deal with them later, because the chances are that it won't be appropriate to deal with them with your clients. *But, do deal with them later.*

Some stories of harassment and bullying can be traumatic even second hand, so be prepared to debrief with your co-workers or your supervisor. Allow them to listen to the story, and the emotional effects it has had on you, and remember that being qualified as counsellors or psychologists does not protect us against traumas such as being bullied ourselves in the past from coming to the surface.

The supervision relationship is one in which dignity and respect can be modelled. This helps the consultant take away an image of how a working alliance can operate. The relationship needs to be honest and open, and it should demonstrate the same core conditions as working as a clinical practitioner. The following suggestions for an alliance model for supervision is adapted from Proctor and Tehrani (2001), quoting Rogers (1961):

- An ability to suspend judgement and put themselves in the shoes of the supervisee/consultant.
- Empathic understanding as the core medium on which the relationship is built
- A willingness to trust and be trustworthy – the supervisor needs to remain impartial and objective even though they are in a position of being removed. They will never meet the perpetrators, the victims or the managers concerned.
- Be prepared to be honest and genuine and offer the space for the supervisee to express their thoughts and feelings in a safe and confidential place, and then look at how they are going to deal with often tricky and disturbing situations.
- The supervisor acts as a second monitor to the supervisee/consultant in terms of their health – physically, psychologically and emotionally.
- The supervisor on hearing the story can act as an objective observer, e.g., is the supervisee/consultant being drawn into the culture and may even be being bullied as part of the process?

The following are some of your own feelings you may have to deal with:

Distress

1 You may identify with the person who has been bullied; it may remind you of a time in your life when you were bulled at school, at work, or in a past relationship. These feelings may surprise you, especially if you have not thought about them for years or would have firmly believed that you had dealt with them.
2 You may feel guilty about the way in which you have treated others in the past and realise that in a place of work that behaviour would no longer be acceptable. Or, you may feel guilty that you have been a bystander watching other people getting bullied and not having the courage to do anything to help them.

Shame

1   As in 2 above, you may feel shame that you behaved in the way you did.
2   You may feel second-hand shame that a member of the same sex, the same race or the same culture as you could have behaved in this way to others.

Frustration

1   You may feel that the wrong person is being punished for the events that have taken place, and that the management is not acting fairly. However, your brief is your brief and you have to remain within it, despite your personal feelings.
2   You have no control over what the management decides to do with the accused, even though, in your opinion, they are clearly in breach of the company policy.
3   Decisions are not always made on what is fair; economics always plays a part. For example, is the person who is accused of bullying more difficult to replace than the victim; does that person make more money for the company; is there a case for constructive dismissal? These are all factors that would not necessarily be discussed with outside professionals yet they have a large role to play in overall decision-making.

Helplessness

You may be feeling helpless that there is nothing you can do to stop this behaviour from happening again. You can counsel, coach, investigate and make recommendations but, ultimately, it is not in your purview to actually make the decisions that can bring an end to the harassment and bullying.

We have to acknowledge that even in 2003, when many companies have policies in place for dealing with inappropriate behaviours, they still go on. Most organisations know exactly what to do if a member of staff is caught defrauding the company in some way, yet many flounder when human beings are being treated badly by others.

Because of these realities, we have to understand and accept that if we intend to work in and with organisations, we have to let go of those things we cannot do anything about.

Taking care of the self is, of course, essential for everyone. How much more so for those who are responsible for the psychological health of others?

Many counsellors, psychologists and supervisors are not familiar with organisations and working in them. Therefore, before taking on this kind of work, check whether your supervisor is happy for you to bring it to them. If not, find a second supervisor who is willing to help supervise, guide and debrief you. It is important that we use our supervisors to debrief us. Many cases have similar flavours to them and, if we don't debrief them individually, they will begin to merge into one in our minds and cause us to suffer stress or even burn-out as a result.

Many of us use checklists when doing assessments on clients. They consist of very basic questions, such as:

- Do you eat healthily?
- Do you get enough sleep to keep you healthy?
- How much alcohol do you drink?
- Do you smoke?
- Do you get enough exercise to keep you healthy?
- Do you have a good support system in your life – do you allow yourself to use it?
- Do you take time off away from your place of work?
- Do you balance your working life with other activities?
- Is your home life an added stressor?
- Do you take 'me' time; i.e., time out to think, to be or to involve yourself in an activity of your choice without having to consider anyone else?

'Me' time is particularly important after finishing a piece of harassment and bullying work. My advice to you is to acknowledge that you did what you could, make sure your invoice has been sent off and, now, let it go!

Diagnostic criteria for 3.09.81 post-traumatic stress disorder

A The person has been exposed to a traumatic event in which both of the following were present:

1 The person experienced, witnessed, or was confronted with an event or events that involved actual or threatened death or serious injury, or a threat to the physical integrity of self or others.

2 The person's response involved intense fear, helplessness, or horror.

B The traumatic event is persistently re-experienced in one (or more) of the following ways:

1 Recurrent and intrusive distressing recollections of the event, including images, thoughts, or perceptions.

2 Recurrent distressing dreams of the event.

3 Acting or feeling as if the traumatic event were recurring (includes a sense of reliving the experience, illusions, hallucinations, and dissociative flashback episodes, including those that occur on awakening or when intoxicated).

4 Intense psychological distress at exposure to internal or external cues that symbolise or resemble an aspect of the traumatic event.

5 Physiological reactivity on exposure to internal or external cues that symbolise or resemble an aspect of the traumatic event.

C Persistent avoidance of stimuli associated with the trauma and numbing of general responsiveness (not present before the trauma), as indicated by three (or more) of the following:

1   efforts to avoid thoughts, feelings, or conversations associated with the trauma;
2   efforts to avoid activities, places, or people that arouse recollections of the trauma;
3   inability to recall an important aspect of the trauma;
4   markedly diminished interest or participation in significant activities;
5   feeling of detachment or estrangement from others;
6   restricted range or affect (e.g. unable to have loving feelings);
7   sense of a foreshortened future (e.g. does not expect to have a career, marriage, children, or a normal life span).

D   Persistent symptoms of increased arousal (not present before the trauma), as indicated by two (or more) of the following:
1   difficulty falling or staying asleep;
2   irritability or outbursts of anger;
3   difficulty concentrating;
4   hypervigilance;
5   exaggerated startle response.

E   Duration of the disturbance (symptoms in criteria B, C, and D) is more than one month.

F   The disturbance causes clinically significant distress or impairment in social, occupational or other important areas of functioning.

For a fuller description of post-traumatic stress disorder, see *Diagnostic and Statistical Manual of Mental Disorders* (1994).

Useful information

Tim Field's website
www.successunlimited.co.uk

Mediation training

P.M.R.
Professional Mediation Resolutions
20 Gaveston Road
Leamington Spa
Warwickshire CV32 6EU
01926 339744
pmr@workplacemediation.co.uk

Training and video materials

Angel Productions
9 Dukes Avenue
London N10 2PS
0208 444 33111
sales@angelproductions.co.uk
www.angelproductions.co.uk

Employee Assistance Professionals Association
Premier House
85 High Street
Witney OX28 5HY

Some consultancies in the field

Leslie Holland
Angel Productions
9 Dukes Avenue
London N10 2PS
0208 444 33111

Linda Hodkinson
Diversity Works
12 Tudor Gardens
Stony Stratford
Milton Keynes MK11 1HX
01908 563 519

Pauline Rennie Peyton
12A Woburn Walk
London WC1H 0JL
0207 387 6528

EAP companies known personally to the author

Coutts Corecare
1631 Parkway
Solent Business Park
Whiteley
Fareham
Hampshire PO15 7AH

Focus Limited
Northside House
Mount Pleasant
Barnet
Herts EN4 9EB
0208 441 9300

Personal Effectiveness Centre
108 Coomb Lane
London SW20 0BR
0208 879 0135
www.pcltd.co.uk

Author's note: There are many other excellent consultants, training organisations and EAP companies. I have listed only people and companies that I have worked with.

Bibliography

Adams, A. with Crawford, N. (1992) *Bullying at Work – How to Confront and Overcome It*, London: Virago.

Adams, A. (1994a) Text of Speech, 24 May 1994, given at a conference sponsored by British Trade Union MSF, online at: www.bullybusters.org/home/twd/bb/bbstudies/adams.html

Adams, A. (1994b) 'The unnecessary evil – bullying at work', *The Therapist*, Summer, p. 16.

Andrea Adams Trust (2000) *The Legal Position on Workplace Bullying*, Brighton: The Andrea Adams Trust.

Archer, D. (1998) *Time to Kill the Culture Vulture*, Divisional Officer David Archer, Hereford and Worcester Fire Brigade.

Ashton, D. (1999) *Managing Employer Liability for Employee Stress*, London, Great Britain, Pearson Education Limited, Financial Times, Prentice-Hall.

Aspinall, P. (2001) 'Is counselling good for business?', *Counselling at Work*, 34: 7–9.

Bagshaw, M. (2000) *Using Emotional Intelligence at Work*, Ely, Cambs: Fenman Training.

Ball, C. (1998) 'Trade union action on bullying at work: the campaign of the professional and technical union', in P. McCarthy *et al.* (eds) *Vital People, Viable Workplaces – Beyond Victimisation*, MSF.

Bassman, E.S. (1992) *Abuse in the Workplace*, Westport, Conn.: Quorum.

Beasley, J. *et al.* (eds) (1997) 'Bullying in adult life', *Journal of Community and Applied Social Psychology*, 7(3): 173–256.

Berne, E. (1961) *Transactional Analysis in Psychotherapy*, New York: Grove Press.

Berne, E. (1963) *The Structure and Dynamics of Organizations and Groups*, New York: Grove Press.

Berne, E. (1966) *Principles of Group Treatment*, New York: Grove Press.

Bjorkqvist, K., Osterman, K. and Hjelt-Back, M. (1994) 'Aggression amongst university employees', *Aggressive Behaviour*, 20: 173–184 (quoted in Petri (1996) unpublished dissertation).

Black, H. (1983) *Black's Law Dictionary* (5th edn), St Paul, Minn.: West.

Bridges, W. (1992) *The Character of Organisations: Using Jungian Type in Organisations*, Palo Alto, Calif.: Consulting Psychologists Press.

Brodsky, C.M. (1976) *The Harassed Worker*, Toronto: Lexington Books, DC Heath & Co.

Butler, C. (1999) 'Organisational counselling: the profession's shadow side', *Counselling*, The Journal of the British Association for Counselling, 10(3): 227–231.

Campbell, D., Coldicott, T. and Kinsella, K. (eds) (1994) *Systemic Work with Organisations*, London: Karnac Books.

Carroll, C. (1997) 'Balancing integration and independence', in L. Macwhinnie (ed.) *An Anthology of Counselling at Work*, Rugby: Association of Counselling at Work.

Carroll, M. (1995) 'The counsellor in organisational settings: some reflections', *Employee Counselling Today*, 7(1): 23–29.

Carroll, M. and Walton, M. (eds) (1997) *Handbook of Counselling in Organisations*, London: Sage.

Clarkson, P. (1989) *Gestalt Counselling in Action*, London: Sage.

Clutterbuck, D. (2002a) *Everyone Needs a Mentor*, CIPD (quoted in J. Whitmore, *Coaching for Performance* (3rd edn), London: Nicholas Brealey).

Clutterbuck, D. (2002b) 'Mentoring executives and directors', *Counselling at Work*, Spring, no. 37, 8–9.

Cockman, P., Evans, B. and Reynolds, P. (1998) *Consulting for Real People* (2nd edn), London: McGraw-Hill International (UK) Limited.

Cooper, C. (1993) 'Finding the solution: primary prevention (identifying the causes and preventing mental ill-health in the workplace)', in R. Jenkins and D. Warman (eds) *Promoting Mental Health Policies in the Workplace*, London: HMSO.

Cooper, C. and Cartwright, S. (1996) *Mental Health and Stress in the Workplace, A Guide for Employers*, London: HMSO.

Cooper, C., Cooper, R. and Eaker, L. (1998) *Living with Stress*, London: Penguin Books.

Cooper, C.L. and Payne, R. (1988) *Causes, Coping and Consequences of Stress at Work*, Chichester: John Wiley & Sons.

Cox, T. (1978) *Stress*, London: Macmillan.

Cox, T. (1993) *Stress Research and Stress Management: Putting Theory to Work*, Centre for Organisational Health and Development, Department of Psychology, University of Nottingham, HSE Contract Research Report No. 6, HMSO.

Coyne, I. *et al.* (2000) 'Personality traits as indicators of workplace bully–victim status', Occupational Psychology Conference, January.

Crawford, N. (1997) 'Bullying at work: a psychoanalytic perspective', *Journal of Community and Applied Social Psychology*, 7: 219–225.

Crawford, N. (1998) 'Understanding the impact of bullying on organisations', Paper presented at the Bullying at Work Litigation conference run by IBC UK Conference Limited.

Crouch, D. (2002) 'Bullies back off', *Nursing Times*, 98(32), 24–27.

Davidson, J., Swartz, M. and Kronenberger, W.J. (1990) 'A diagnostic and family study of post-traumatic stress disorder', *American Journal of Psychiatry*, 142: 90–93.

de Villere, M.F. (1981) *Transactional Analysis at Work*, Englewood Cliffs, N.J.: Prentice-Hall.

Diagnostic and Statistical Manual of Mental Disorders, Fourth Edition – DSM–IV^{TM} (1994) Washington, DC: American Psychiatric Association.

Doherty, N. (1998) 'Mediation in the workplace', *Training Officer*, 34(8): 5–6.

Earnshaw, J. and Cooper, C. (1996) *Stress and Employer Liability*, London: Institute of Personnel and Development.

Egan, G. (1994) *Working the Shadow Side*, San Francisco: Jossey-Bass.

Einarssen, S. and Skogstad, A. (1996) 'Epidemiological findings of bullying', *European Journal of Work and Organisational Psychology*, 5(2): 185–201.

Einarssen, S., Raknes, B.I. and Matthiesen, S.B. (1994) 'Bullying and its relationship to work and environment quality: an exploratory study', *European Work & Organisational Psychologist*, 4: 381–401.

English, F. (1975) 'The three cornered contract', *The Transactional Analysis Journal*, 5(4): 383–384.

Erskine, R.G. (1999) *Beyond Empathy – A Therapy of Contact in Relationships*, London: Brunner/Mazel.

Evarts, W.R., Greenstone, J.L., Kilpatrick, G. and Leviton, S.C. (1983) *Winning Through Accommodation: The Mediator's Handbook*, Dubuque, Ia.: Kendall/Hunt.

Field, T. (1996) *Bully in Sight*, Wantage: Wessex Press.

Field, T. (1998) 'What is the cost to the employer of bullying?', Paper presented at Bullying at Work Litigation conference run by IBC UK Conference Limited, London, 19 May.

Field, T. (2001) Bully On Line, website of UK National Bullying Advice Line, at www.successunlimited.co.uk

Findlay, Z. and Reynolds, C. (1997) *The Workplace Mediation Manual*, London: Hilltop.

Firth, D. and Leigh, A. (1998) *The Corporate Fool*, Oxford: Capstone Publishing.

Galen, M. (1991) 'Is Big Blue hostile to grey hairs?', *Business Week*, October 21: 33–34.

Garrett, T. (1997) 'Trainer–Trainee Bullying', *Journal of Community and Applied Social Psychology*, 7: 227–232.

Goleman, D. (1996) *Emotional Intelligence*, London: Bloomsbury.

Greenhalgh, V. (1999) 'Don't suffer in silence – beat the office bully', *The Times*, October 27.

Groeblinghoff, D. and Becker, M. (1996) 'A case study of mobbing and the clinical treatment of mobbing victims', *European Journal of Work and Organisational Psychology*, 5(2): 251–275.

Hay, J. (1996 [1988]) *Transactional Analysis for Trainers*, Watford: Sherwood Publishing.

Hirschhorn, L. (1997) *The Workplace Within*, Boston, Mass.: MIT Press.

Hoel, H. and Cooper, C.L. (2000) 'Destructive conflict and bullying at work', Sponsored by the British Occupational Health Research Foundation (BOHRF), Manchester School of Management, Manchester University of Science and Technology (UMIST).

Hofstede, G. (1991) *Cultures and Organisations: Software of the Mind*, Maidenhead: McGraw-Hill International (UK) Limited.

Holland, L. (1998) – adapted from course material, Angel Productions (see Useful Information, Appendix II).

Ishmael, A. (1999) *Harassment, Bullying and Violence at Work*, London: The Industrial Society.

Jenkins, P. and Pollecoff, P. (2000) 'Opportunities for workplace counselling to minimise the threat of litigation', *Counselling at Work*, 30: 7–9.

Johnson, R.A. (1993) *Owning Your Own Shadow: Understanding the Dark Side of the Psyche*, New York: HarperCollins.

Karpman, S. (1968) 'Drama triangle: fairy tales and script drama analysis', *Transactional Analysis Bulletin*, 7(26): 39–43.

Kerr, S. (1998) 'Integrity in effective leadership', in S. Srivastva and Associates (eds) *Executive Integrity: The Search for High Human Values in Organisational Life*, San Francisco: Jossey-Bass.

Kompier, M. and Levi, L. (1994) 'Stress at work: does it concern you?', *European Foundation for the Improvement of Living and Working Conditions*, EF/94/21/EN, Luxembourg: Office for Official Publications of the European Communities.

Landsberg, M. (1997) *The Tao of Coaching*, London: HarperCollins Business.

Lane, D.A. (1990) 'Counselling psychology in organisations', *The Psychologist: Bulletin of the British Psychological Society*, 12: 540–544.

Lawrence, C. (2001) 'Social psychology of bullying in the workplace', in N. Tehrani (ed.) *Building a Culture of Respect: Managing Bullying at Work*, London and New York: Taylor & Francis.

Leather, P., Brady, C., Lawrence, C., Beale, D. and Cox, T. (eds) (1999)

Work-Related Violence Assessment and Intervention, London and New York: Routledge.

Leviton, S.C. and Greenstone, J.L. (1997) *Elements of Mediation*, Pacific Grove, Calif.: Brooks/Cole Publishing Company.

Leymann, H. (1990) 'Mobbing and psychological terror at workplaces', *Violence and Victims*, 5(2): 119–125.

Leymann, H. (1993) 'Ätiolgie under Häufigkeit von Mobbing am Arbeitsplatz – eine Übersicht über die bisherige Forschung', *Zeitschrift über Personalforschung*, 7: 271–284.

Leymann, H. (1996) 'The content and development of mobbing at work', *European Journal of Work and Organisational Psychology*, 5(2): 165–184.

Lyons, R. (2001) Press release 'Britain's vilest employer caught by long arm of the union', 10 September.

McDonald, L. (2000) 'Bullying at work hits one in four women', *Daily Express*, October 9.

McLeod, J. and McLeod, J. (2001) 'How effective is workplace counselling? A review of workplace literature', *Counselling and Psychotherapy Research*, 1(3): 184–190.

Mead (2001) Press release, Associated Press June 2001.

MENCAP – Survey commissioned by. 'Campaigning for rights and respect'. Press release from *Press Association*, Jones, T, June 2001.

Menzies Lyth, I. (1988) 'Containing anxiety in institutions', *Selected Essays*, Vol. 1, London: Free Association Books, pp. 43–88.

Mindell, A. (1995) *Sitting in the Fire*, Portland, Oreg.: Lao Tse Press.

Morgan, G. (1986) *Images of Organisation*, Newbury, Calif.: Sage.

MSF Health and Safety Office (1995) *Bullying at Work: How To Tackle It*, Bishop's Stortford: College Hill Press.

National Workplace Bullying Advice Line www.successunlimited.co.uk/action/dignity.htm

Nevis, E.C. (1987) *Organisational Consulting*, New York: Gestalt Institute of Cleveland Press.

Niedl, K. (1995) *Mobbing/Bullying am Arbeitsplatz*, Muenchen und Mering: Rainer Hampp Verlag.

Novey, T.B. (1976) *TA for Management*, Sacramento, Calif.: JALMAR Press Inc.

Oberhardt, M. (1998) 'Worker awarded $500,000', *The Courier-Mail*, 24 April.

Obholzer, A. and Roberts, V.Z. (eds) (1994) *The Unconscious at Work: Individual and Organisational Stress in the Human Services*, London: Routledge.

Orlans, V. and Edwards, D. (2001) 'Counselling the organisation', *Counselling at Work*, Summer, no. 33: 5.

Pearson, C. (1999) 'Workplace Incivility Study', online at www.bullbus-ters.org/home/twd/bb/res/pearson.html

Peltier, B. (2001) *The Psychology of Executive Coaching*, New York: Brunner-Routledge.

Petri, H. (1996) 'Lucky to have a job?', Unpublished MA dissertation, University of Middlesex.

Petri, H. (1997) 'Lucky to have a job?', in V. Merchant (ed.) *Conference of the National Harassment Network Higher and Future Education Branch*.

Petri, H. (1998) 'The road to ruin', Paper presented at the Bullying at Work Conference, Staffordshire University, Stafford.

Proctor, B. and Tehrani, N. (2001) 'Issues for counsellors and supporters', in N. Tehrani (ed.) *Building a Culture of Respect: Managing Bullying at Work*, London: Taylor & Francis.

Randall, P. (1997) *Adult Bullying Perpetrators and Victims*, London and New York: Routledge.

Rayner, C. (1997) 'The incidence of workplace bullying', *Journal of Community and Applied Social Psychology*, 7: 199–208.

Rayner, C. (1998a) 'What is bullying? How widespread is it? Why is it happening?', Paper presented at the Bullying at Work Litigation conference run by IBC UK Conferences Limited.

Rayner, C. (1998b) 'From research to implementation: finding leverage for intervention and prevention', Paper presented at the Bullying at Work 1998 Research Update Conference, Staffordshire University Business School, 1 July.

Rayner, C. and Hoel, H. (1997) 'A summary review of literature relating to workplace bullying', *Journal of Community and Applied Social Psychology*, 7: 181–191.

Rayner, C., Hoel, H. and Cooper, C.L. (2002) *Workplace Bullying*, London and New York: Taylor & Francis.

Read, J. and Baker, S. (1996) 'Not just sticks and stones: a survey of the stigma, taboos and discrimination experienced by people with mental health problems', London: MIND.

Reynolds, C. (2000) 'Workplace mediation', in M. Liebmann (ed.) *Mediation in Context*, London: Jessica Kingsley Publishers Ltd.

Rigby, K. (2002) *New Perspectives on Bullying*, London: Jessica Kingsley Publishers Limited.

Robinson, J. (1999) 'Profession plagued by blight of bullying', *Personnel Today*, 5 August: 1.

Rogers, C. (1961) *On Becoming a Person*, Boston: Houghton Mifflin.

Rose, W. (2001) 'Exploring the shadow of an organisation', *Counselling at Work*, 35: 6–8.

Samuels, A., Shorter, B. and Plaut, F. (1986) *A Critical Dictionary of Jungian Analysis*, London: Routledge.

Savva, C. (1997) 'An investigation and analysis of the impact of bullying in Further and Higher Education and the implementation of a system to combat the problem', Dissertation for MA in Employment Studies and Human Resource Management, University of North London.

Schiff, J. *et al.* (1975) *The Cathexis Reader: Transactional Analysis Treatment of Psychosis*, New York: Harper & Row.

Seward, K. (1998) 'Dignity at work: the law on bullying (and harassment) in the workplace', Paper presented at the Bullying at Work Litigation conference run by IBC UK Conferences Limited.

Seyle, H. (1956) *The Stress of Life*, New York: McGraw-Hill.

Seyle, H. (1974) *Stress Without Distress*, Philadelphia, Pa.: J.B. Lippincott.

Sharp, S. and Smith, P.K. (1994) *Tackling Bullying in Your School – A Practical Handbook for Teachers*, London: Routledge.

Sheehan, M. (1998) 'Bullying – signs and solutions'. School of Organisational Behaviour and Human Resource Management, Griffith University, Australia. Paper presented at the Bullying at Work Research Update Conference.

Smith, P.K. and Sharp, S. (1994) *School Bullying: Insights and Perspectives*, London: Routledge.

Smithers, R. (2001) 'Bullying at heart of British culture', *The Guardian*, 6 November.

Stapley, L.F. (1996) *The Personality of the Organisation: A Psycho-Dynamic Explanation of Culture and Change*, London: Free Association Books.

Steiner, C. (1984) 'Emotional literacy', *The Transactional Analysis Journal*, 14(3): 162–173.

Steiner, C. (1990) *Scripts People Live*, Nottingham: Bantam Books.

Stewart, I. and Joines, V. (1987) *TA Today: A New Introduction to Transactional Analysis*, Nottingham: Lifespace Publishing.

Sutton, J. (2001) 'Bullies: thugs or thinkers?', *The Psychologist*, 14(10): 530–534.

Tehrani, N. (ed.) (2001) *Building a Culture of Respect: Managing Bullying at Work*, London and New York: Taylor & Francis.

Tehrani, N. (2002) Survey results presented at Working Together, a British Association for Counselling and Psychotherapy Conference, 17–18 May.

Towler, J. (1997) 'Managing the counselling process in organisations', in M. Carroll and M. Walton (eds) *Handbook of Counselling in Organisations*, London: Sage.

Trade Union Congress (TUC) (1998) Conference, 5 October.

Turner, S. and Davies, S. (2000) 'EAPs and work/life programs: solutions to the whole puzzle', *EAP Association Exchange: The Magazine of the Employee Assistance Professionals Association*, 30(5): 21–23.

Vartia, M. (1996) 'The sources of bullying – psychological work environment and organisational climate', *European Journal of Work Organisational Psychology*, 5(2): 203–214.

Von Eckardstein, D., Lueger, G., Niedl, K. and Schuster, B. (1995) *Psychische Befindensbeeintrachtigung und Gesundheit im Betrieb. Herausforderung für Personnalmanager under Gesundheitsexperten*, Munchen: Rainer Hampp Verlag.

Wagner, A. (1991) *The Transactional Manager*, Denver, Colo.: T.A. Communications Inc.

Weisinger, H. (1998) *Emotional Intelligence at Work*, San Francisco: Jossey-Bass.

Whitmore, J. (2002) *Coaching for Performance* (3rd edn), London: Nicholas Brealey.

Will, D. and Rate, R. (1985) *Integrated Family Therapy*, London: Tavistock Publications.

Wright, L. and Smye, M. (1997) *Corporate Abuse*, New York: Simon & Schuster.

Zapf, D., Knorz, C. and Kulla, M. (1995) 'Causes and consequences of various mobbing factors at work', Paper presented at the Symposium, 7th European Congress of Work and Organisational Psychology, Gyor, Hungary.

Zapf, D. and Leymann, H. (eds) (1996) 'Mobbing and victimisation at work', *The European Journal of Work and Organisational Psychology*, Special Issue, 5(2).

Index

Note: page numbers in **bold** refer to diagrams.